WHEN YOUR Soulmate Dies

A GUIDE TO HEALING THROUGH HEROIC MOURNING

ALAN D. WOLFELT, PH.D.

Companion
PRESS

An imprint of the Center for Loss and Life Transition
Fort Collins, Colorado

Companion
PRESS

Companion Press is dedicated to the education and support of both the bereaved and bereavement caregivers. We believe that those who companion the bereaved by walking with them as they journey in grief have a wondrous opportunity: to help others embrace and grow through grief—and to lead fuller, more deeply lived lives themselves because of this important ministry.

For a complete catalog and ordering information, write, call, or visit us at the address below, 970.226.6050, www.centerforloss.com.

Companion Press is an imprint of the Center for Loss and Life Transition, 3735 Broken Bow Road, Fort Collins, Colorado, 80526.

25   24   23   6

ISBN 978-1-61722-242-9

*I dedicate this book to the grieving soulmates who
so bravely and generously shared their stories of
soulmate love and loss with me and with you, the reader.
In these pages your epic love and grief will be forever honored.*

IN REMEMBRANCE OF

Adam	Deb	Judy	Rebecca
Allen	Don	Julene	Rick
Barbara	Edwin	Kathryn Anne	Ron
Bart	Frank	Larry	Sharon
Benjie	Gary	Lee	Steve
Bob	George	Les	Stu
Bryan	Janell	Libby	Tim
Cliff	Jeanne	Mark	Warren
Dan	Jerry	Michael	Wendell
Darren	Jim	Mike	
Dave	Joan	Patrick	
David	John	Philip	

And all soulmates whose lives made ours so meaningful

ALSO BY DR. ALAN WOLFELT

The Depression of Grief:
Coping with Your Sadness and Knowing When to Get Help

Grief One Day at a Time:
365 Meditations to Help You Heal After Loss

Healing a Spouse's Grieving Heart:
100 Practical Ideas After Your Husband or Wife Dies

The Journey Through Grief: Reflections on Healing

Loving from the Outside In, Mourning from the Inside Out

The Paradoxes of Mourning:
Healing Your Grief with Three Forgotten Truths

Understanding Your Grief:
Ten Essential Touchstones for
Finding Hope and Healing Your Heart

To order and for more information on Dr. Wolfelt's books,
visit www.centerforloss.com.

CONTENTS

PREFACE

In my four decades as a grief student, teacher, and counselor, I have met and walked alongside thousands of mourners. In sharing their stories of love and loss, they have taught me so much about their unique perspectives and needs. Throughout my career I have tried to pass along their messages of hope and healing.

To that end, I have written many articles and books—and given thousands of presentations—on grief. We live in a grief-avoidant culture, and I believe that if I use my time here on earth to share the hard-earned wisdom mourners have imparted to me along the way, I am living my calling. I am a conduit and spokesperson. Those who have learned to mourn well want to help those struggling with grief. I humbly serve as their middleman of sorts.

And so, to offer targeted, relevant assistance as much as possible, I have taught and written about a wide variety of types of loss. On my website you will find targeted books for people grieving in the aftermath of suicide, PTSD, divorce, and the death of a child, parent, or adult sibling, as well as many other losses.

In this vein, 13 years ago I wrote a small book entitled *Healing a Spouse's Grieving Heart: 100 Practical Ideas After Your Husband or Wife Dies.* Part of my *100 Ideas* series, it speaks to the unique qualities of grief and needs of mourning faced by widows and widowers young and old. Since then, tens of thousands of grieving spouses and life partners have held *Healing a Spouse's Grieving Heart* in their hands, and if the online reviews and letters I receive are to be believed, quite a number have been helped by it. For that I am grateful.

Are you sensing a "but" in the offing? If so, you are right. During the decade-plus that *Healing a Spouse's Grieving Heart* has been in print, I have received numerous comments, emails, and entreaties from a group of mourners who believe that it does not adequately address their needs. They tell me that they lost not only a husband, wife, life partner, or sometimes a different special person with whom they had a deep connection, such as a parent, child, or friend—they lost a soulmate.

The soulmate's grief is unique, they taught me. It is more profound and pervasive. It is more akin to the death of a twin. It is the severing of a timeless relationship, one possibly formed before life here on earth.

Then inevitably they would ask: Would you please write a book about the death of a soulmate? Yes, I finally replied when my writing schedule allowed. Yes, I will relate what you have taught me about the grief that follows the death of a soulmate. I will share your true, personal stories. I will also pass along your guidance about how to honor the soulmate who died and go on to live and love well again.

Grieving soulmates of the world, this book is for you. I hope it helps open you to an ever-growing measure of affirmation, hope, and healing.

INTRODUCTION

No doubt you come to this book with a broken heart. You may have noticed that the paper heart on this book's cover stands in empathy with your inner reality—torn in half and ripped ragged. So I would like to begin by saying I am genuinely sorry for your loss.

"Whatever our souls are made of, his and mine are the same."

— Emily Brontë

While mere words—written or spoken—cannot take away the devastation you feel, they do have the power to foster expression and understanding. And while I realize that human language is woefully inadequate at capturing the relationship you had with the precious person who died and the grief you now experience, it is the communication tool we have at our disposal, you and I.

So, when words are sometimes inadequate in the following pages, when they fall short or miss their mark for you—which they can't help but do at times, given the profoundly special, unique, and intimate relationship you had with your soulmate—I hope you will have grace, skip the passages that don't resonate, and continue reading. We are all of us doing our best to help one another.

WHAT IS A SOULMATE?

I have come to understand that the word "soulmate" means different things to different people. Most of us agree that soulmates are two people who feel a deep affinity for and closeness with one another. They are usually lovers and spouses or life partners—but not always. Soulmates are sometimes parent and child, siblings, or close friends. In fact, how society labels or views the relationship from the outside is of little consequence. What matters is the strength and qualities of the bond in the relationship as experienced from inside it. The shorthand soulmates often use to describe one another is "the love of my life."

SOULMATES OTHER THAN SPOUSES OR LIFE PARTNERS

Soulmates are any two souls who share a particularly deep affinity. Sue and several other people who wrote to me about their soulmate experiences know someone other than a spouse or life partner to have been their soulmate.

> *"I know my mom was my soulmate. I felt her in every fiber of my being. I would have done anything for her."*
>
> — Sue Merritt

For Marni Geissler, it was her best friend, who also happened to be a priest: "When I prepared his death notice, I wondered how to list myself," wrote Marni. "I was not part of his biological family, although my siblings and their children had adopted John. 'Soulmate' was the most honest word I could think of."

For Sharon Triano-Kott, it was her best friend, Barbara: "I met Barbara over 40 years ago, when we were both single parents with our children in a home daycare center. We immediately bonded. We remained soulmates and shared hopes, dreams, birthdays, holidays, birth, sickness, and death."

For Penny Blazej, it was her daughter, Kathryn Anne: "She came into my life in early spring, when the daffodils were in bloom, and died in February, when the snow covered the ground and the trees were bare. During her 11 months on earth she taught me more about life than anyone before or after."

From these examples we can see that any two people can be soulmates. Because soulmate as spouse or life partner is the most common soulmate relationship, you will find it used as the default type or example throughout most of this book. If you are a grieving soulmate from a different kind of relationship, however, please know that I welcome you to this conversation. Feel free to skip over any particulars that don't apply to you, and use what does. While the details may not always suit, I believe you will find the general principles helpful.

Beyond this understanding of the fundamental nature of the soulmate relationship are various other criteria that enjoy less of a consensus. For example, some people believe that soulmates are predestined to be together. For them, it's a question of fate and love at first sight. Conversely, others hold that soulmates are not born but rather made. In their view, people who come together in a relationship may grow into soulmates over time as they weather life's many storms and learn to trust, support, and selflessly love one another. Many of the people who wrote to me about their soulmate stories seem to consider their relationships a mixture of both—an initial strong attraction or crush that over time developed into truer and truer love.

> *"I feel like a part of my soul has loved you since the beginning of everything. Maybe we're from the same star."*
>
> — Emery Allen

Similarly, some people think that soulmates are always in sync and get along like two peas in a pod, while others insist that soulmate relationships can be rocky and fiery because soulmates constantly challenge one another. "People think a soulmate is your perfect fit," writes Elizabeth Gilbert in *Eat, Pray, Love*. "But a true soulmate is a mirror... A soulmate's purpose is to shake you up, tear apart your ego a little bit...break your heart open so new light can get in."

Whether or not soulmates are rare is another facet of the concept that entertains a number of viewpoints. Some people believe that there is just one soulmate for each of us. Others think that we may have several soulmates in a lifetime. And, as I mentioned above, still others posit that soulmates don't come ready-made but are instead created—forged of commitment and time lived together.

In this last view, potential soulmates may abound because more ordinary relationships can grow into soulmate relationships over time through the alchemy of love, selflessness, kindness, and shared experience.

I would be remiss here if I did not also mention our culture's tendency to be cynical about the idea of soulmates. You may have encountered people along the way who don't believe in it or who scoff at it. Others judge soulmate relationships as overly intertwined or codependent. As with so many things in life, it can be hard for people to understand something they themselves have never experienced. Rest assured that this book is a safe place for exploring soulmate grief. Not only do I believe that the soulmate attachment is unique and very real, I feel honored to facilitate this exploration.

You might be interested to know that Plato wrote about one version of the concept of soulmates all the way back in the year 380 B.C. In his mythological text *Symposium*, he says that human beings originally had two faces, four arms, and four legs. They lived in joy because they were happy and complete. But then jealous Zeus came along and split them in two, and ever since, people have spent their lives searching for their other halves. (More on the idea of the "other half" on page 9.)

SECRET SOULMATE RELATIONSHIPS

Some soulmates find themselves in a relationship that for various reasons can't be revealed to the outside world. When one soulmate in such a private partnership dies, the surviving soulmate's grief may become disenfranchised—in other words, unacknowledged and unsupported. If you are a grieving "secret soulmate," I urge you to identify a friend and/ or grief counselor with whom it is safe to honestly share your story and the depth of your thoughts and feelings. Secret grief is too great a burden to bear by yourself. You, too, need and deserve ongoing empathy and support.

The term itself—soulmate—wasn't coined until 1822, by the English poet Samuel Taylor Coleridge. Since then both the word and the idea have increasingly captured our collective imaginations. Hundreds of nonfiction books, novels, movies, artworks, and songs have celebrated the possibility. We are in love with the promise, potential, and, when we are lucky enough to encounter it, experience of a soulmate relationship.

When I began to work on this book, I asked a number of grieving soulmates I've had the privilege of meeting during my travels and teaching to tell me what *they* mean by "soulmate." You will find their responses scattered throughout the remainder of this chapter. In the chapters to come I will draw on more of their examples and wisdom. When it comes to healing in grief, fellow travelers who have experienced the same type of loss are often able to provide the most helpful affirmations and counsel. I'm so grateful that they have shared their stories with me so I can share them with you.

WHAT ABOUT THE "SOUL" IN "SOULMATE"?

The term "soulmate" is so commonly used today that we ourselves might employ it without really considering its spiritual connotations. But I find that when I ask, it becomes apparent that many—but not all—people who believe in the idea of soulmates also believe in the idea of the soul.

The soul is generally thought to be the part of ourselves that is eternal. It is separate from our bodies, which are earthbound and live and die. However, it is our souls that animate, or give life to, our bodies. Our souls existed before we were born and continue to exist after we die.

> *"There is a connectedness between the two of you, and you feel closer to them than you have to any other person you have met. There is a peace, a calmness, a deep joy and happiness. When you are around them, life seems more beautiful. It is a feeling of belonging and deep love."*
>
> — Patricia Gardiner

For millennia, most religions have relied, at least in part, on the concept of the soul. Lots of today's spiritual thinkers are equally invested in the idea. Deepak Chopra says that the soul is the core of our being and transcends space and time. Eckhart Tolle echoes that the soul is our innermost being and essence. And author Daniel Pink has weighed in with this definition: "The soul is our capacity to see that our lives are about something more than simply the day to day, and that we're here for a purpose. It could be connected to religion or not, but that there is a purpose of your being here."

"We did everything together and were always so in sync. It felt effortless being together, and we had so many things in common."

— Victoria Muñoz-Schmitt

Some religions and spiritual thinkers go further by making a distinction between the soul and the spirit. The Bible teaches that the soul consists of the mind, the will, and the emotions, while the spirit is eternal and divine. In keeping with this understanding, the Christian theologian Thomas Moore says that the soul is attached to the sensory reality of what happens in everyday life, and the spirit is the aspect of the self that seeks universal, eternal connection and understanding. Spiritual thinker Ram Dass, too, thinks that spirit transcends soul. For our purposes in this book, however, the potential distinction between soul and spirit is overly esoteric. So I will instead combine the concepts of soul and spirit and use the terms interchangeably in the pages to come.

"I knew he was my soulmate because we had so many similar experiences and we shared so many inner thoughts with each other."

— Joanne Churilla

Soulmates, then, are two people who connect on the level of the soul. Those who believe in predestination may go so far as to claim that soulmates are two souls who, before being born into human bodies, agreed in advance to connect with one another here on earth. They may have decided to join together for companionship or to help each other fulfill their separate destinies, and they will reunite again after both bodies have died. Those who believe in reincarnation go one step further, maintaining that soulmates are people whose existences have intersected in significant ways in past lives. Their souls have long been connected—perhaps for many centuries. They continue to come together as soulmates in each new incarnation—whatever that may be—because they have more work to do together.

> "We did life together—the good, the hard, the daily stuff. We traveled. Our shoulders pressed together during concerts, weddings, and funerals of loved ones. Each night we held each other tightly and prayed together as we drifted off to sleep. Through the years our souls were woven together to become more than one."
>
> — Debra Milligan

Where do I stand on the question of souls? I received my core religious teachings growing up in the Methodist church, and I seek to be a spiritual being here on this earth. I am open to the mystery of the immortal soul and know that grief is, at bottom, a soul-based journey.

WELCOME TO THE CONVERSATION

Whatever particulars you may or may not believe about eternal souls, if you are reading this book, I assume you probably feel at least some affinity for the general concept. On the other hand, one of the people who wrote to me about their soulmate losses, Beverley Turnley, said that she prefers the term "lifemate" over "soulmate" because neither she nor her husband, Frank, considered themselves spiritual people. So regardless of where you find yourself on the continuum of the question of souls and soulmates, I'm glad you've found this book, and I welcome you to our conversation. I believe we have much to learn from each other.

This is another concept that often shapes people's understanding of what it means to be a soulmate. Couples often talk about their "other half" or their "better half." There is also a belief—both sacramental and secular—that two become one through marriage.

Similarly, in addition to the word "soulmate," you may sometimes hear the term "twin flames" applied to extraordinarily close relationships. In fact, some believe that this is the most special and rare form of relationship. In twin flames, the story goes, a single soul divided into two before birth and now inhabits two people. When these two people meet one another on earth, there is an instant recognition and feelings of joy and bliss as well as a sense of wholeness. While soulmates are partners, twin flames are one being.

I respect whatever you believe about soulmates, the soul, other halves, and twin flames. However *you* define soulmate is correct, at least for you. Your reality is your reality. Your relationship with the person who died was one-of-a-kind. If you believe you were soulmates, you were soulmates. I am not meeting you here on this page to ask you to pass some kind of a soulmate test. I'm here to help you find the courage and path to embrace your uniquely debilitating grief and find meaning in life again.

> *"Not only did we share common values and goals but also dreams. I learned early on in my marriage that I had to be very careful of what I asked for because he would make it happen. We shared a love of creating family, a beautiful home, artful projects, sharing times with friends. We just knew that we were meant to be together, and that as a whole we were far greater than the sum of the parts."*
>
> — Julie Lynn McIntyre

WHAT IS GRIEF?

Now that we've considered the various understandings and nuances of what it means to be a soulmate, I'd also like to explore the other two foundational terms that are essential to our conversation in this book: "grief" and "mourning."

Grief is everything we think and feel inside after someone or something we care about is taken away from us. Grief can be sadness. Grief can be anger. Grief can be shock and regret and confusion. Grief can be these and many other possible emotions and thoughts. When we are grieving, precisely which mixture of emotions and thoughts we have inside of us changes from moment to moment and day to day.

"I knew this was a soulmate relationship since I felt unconditional love when I was around her, complete understanding and empathy, and a wholeness that our souls had connected."

— Sharon Triano-Kott

In general, though, the stronger our attachment to the someone or something that was taken away from us, the stronger our grief. Obviously, we grieve more deeply when a loved one dies than an acquaintance, for example. Because the soulmate relationship is by definition built upon a particularly strong attachment, the grief that follows the tearing-apart of that relationship is also particularly strong.

SOULMATE GRIEF

You have no doubt experienced a number of losses in your life, big and small. How has your grief in the aftermath of the death of your soulmate compared to the grief you felt after other losses?

I asked my readers to weigh in on this question, and here are some of their poignant responses:

*"In prior years I had experienced profound grief, but the loss of my soulmate, though not sudden or unexpected, was **overpowering and much harder for me to process**. It has **turned my life completely upside down** in so many ways that I cannot even begin to describe."*

— John Sammons after the death of his wife, Libby

"The grief when she died was different from all others I have experienced. I had survived the loss of parents, grandparents,

aunts, and uncles to whom I was very connected, yet still I had remained whole. *This loss left me in broken pieces, crumbling and wondering how I could go on.*"

— Sharon Triano-Kott after the death of her best friend, Barbara

"*I remember feeling numb when my father passed away when I was 12, when my brother passed away when I was 30, and when my mother passed away when I was 40. The death of Gary was* **worse than I could ever have imagined.** *Gary and I had always said we wanted to go to heaven together. He left without me.*"

— Jo Anne Gregory after the death of her husband

"*His death left me in shock. This grief was unlike that experienced with our parents and dear friends. The main difference for me was a feeling of devastation.*"

— Linda Albright after the death of her husband, Bob

"*There was no comparison to the other losses in my life. When Steve died,* **I felt as if I had been run over by a truck—repeatedly.** *I was shocked at how deep the hurt was.*"

— Rita Roush, after the death of her husband

"*In searching for a word that describes my inner-self following my wife's death, my word is* **fractured.**"

— Don Mueller, after the death of his wife, Janell

"**The grief felt lethal.**"

— James Cox, after the death of his wife, Sharon

Perhaps you recognize the depth and severity of your own grief thoughts and feelings in the descriptions these grieving soulmates have shared with us. They are affirming that the grief they experienced in the aftermath of the death of their soulmates was much more devastating than other griefs they encountered in their lives.

We'll be talking more about the unique nature and amplitude of

> *"The saying 'You don't know what you have till it's gone' rings true for me. I didn't really discover that my husband was my soulmate until after his passing. We thought we had all the time in the world, but we didn't."*
>
> — Kathy Chandler

soulmate grief in the following chapters, but for now I just want you to know that I believe and empathize with you. I understand that your grief is excruciatingly painful and hard—maybe the most challenging thing you have ever experienced in your entire life. I am sorry that you are suffering. I hope that as we move forward together in this book, you will find your way toward a measure of hope of healing.

SOULMATE GRIEF AS COMPLICATED GRIEF

I've said that whenever something or someone we care about is taken away from us, we grieve inside. Our grief is the natural and necessary response to loss. It is innate. It is normal.

> *"I know without looking in the dictionary that we were soulmates, not necessarily from the beginning of our relationship, but definitely we found true happiness through the intimacy, compatibility, spirituality, and love we shared with one another and our family and friends."*
>
> — John Sammons

But sometimes the circumstances of the loss make our grief especially challenging. In such situations, our normal grief often becomes oversized and overwhelming. We have what I deem a normal response to an abnormally difficult loss. In other words, our grief becomes complicated.

Here are just some of the circumstances that can give rise to complicated grief:

- sudden and/or violent and/or lingering death
- premature death
- additional significant life stressors at the same time
- lack of support systems

- stigmatized losses (such as suicide)

In the case of the death of a soulmate, it is the nature of the relationship with the person who died that can be seen as a complicating factor. Your intensely close relationship to your soulmate—possibly in addition to other complicating factors, such as sudden death or a background in which grief was shamed or ignored—has made your grief complicated. The more dependent you were on your partner emotionally, financially, physically, or in other ways, the more complicated your grief is likely to be. The more the two of you isolated yourselves from others, the more complicated your grief is likely to be. The more you saw yourself as half of a whole instead of an independent individual, the more complicated your grief is likely to be. The more you dedicated your time to caring for your soulmate, the more complicated your grief is likely to be.

> *"He was not only my husband but my best friend, my lover, father of our children, my partner in crime, my main supporter, but most of all part of who I was. It's always been Stu and Marsha. I couldn't even think how it would now be just Marsha."*
>
> — Marsha Pettigrew

Rest assured that none of this means there is something wrong with you or your soulmate relationship. All of these factors come into play because they are facets of attachment, and as we have said, the stronger the attachment, the stronger the grief. The term "complicated grief" simply takes into account that your grief is proportionate to the magnitude and circumstances of your loss. As a grieving soulmate, you are likely having a normal grief reaction to an abnormally severe loss borne of an unusually strong attachment.

And people who experience complicated grief—whatever its cause—often need a little more help along the way.

You might think of complicated grief as a grave psychic injury. How do we care for people who sustain life-threatening physical injuries?

We place them in special wings of the hospital called intensive care units. In the ICU, they receive extra care of all kinds—a single nurse who cares only for them, more physician oversight, breathing support, etc. The more complicated your grief, the more you deserve the emotional and spiritual equivalent of the ICU. Be extra gentle and patient with yourself, and seek out all the support you need.

> *"How did I know it was a soulmate relationship? I think I knew because I never asked myself this question. He was part of my soul, and there was never a time when he wasn't. None of us can see our face unless we look in a mirror. We just know it's there and always has been."*
>
> — Pat Lillicrop

WHAT IS MOURNING?

If your grief is everything you have felt and thought inside since the death of your soulmate, then what is mourning? Mourning is what happens when you let your grief out. In other words, mourning is the external expression of your grief.

When you cry, you are mourning. When you talk to others about your grief or about memories of your soulmate who died, you are mourning. When you write in a journal, pray, or look through old photo albums, you are mourning. Essentially, anything you do to engage with your inner thoughts and feelings and connect them to someone or something *out there* in the world is mourning.

Mourning, as we will discuss in the coming chapters, gives your excruciating grief movement. Over time and with the support of others, it is mourning that will soften your grief and help you find renewed meaning in life. To mourn is to heal.

AN INVITATION TO PERSONALIZE YOUR EXPERIENCE

You will notice that each of the chapters in this book contains questions based on the chapter's content as well as space for you to write out your answers. I invite you to spend some time thinking and writing before you move on to the next chapter. Many grievers find this method of mourning their grief extremely helpful. It's as if each time they share a small part of their story by writing it down, they take one small step toward self-understanding and healing. If you are skeptical about the idea of writing about your grief, or if you are someone who would normally not give it a try, I urge you to complete at least the first set of questions and answers and see what happens.

> *"It was like that piece of music that just touches you in a special way. The first time I met him I became emotionally touched and tearful. There was something in his eyes, his smile, and his sense of kindness that somehow stirred up a wild and wonderful response in the depth of my soul. I just knew he was 'the one.'"*
>
> — Maureen Kreutzmann

> *"A soulmate is someone you want to spend forever with."*
>
> — Susan Robison

Yet I do realize there are those among you who, for various reasons, will not put pen to paper. For you, a good alternative to writing may be to talk through the questions and answers with a good listener—perhaps even someone else who has experienced a similar loss. Writing and talking are equally valid forms of mourning, with the latter having the added benefit of the empathy of a fellow human being.

Before we move on, I would also like to suggest that some of you may not be ready to continue with this exploration at this time. Depending on how long ago your soulmate died, depending on the difficulty of your grief journey so far, depending on the support systems around you and many other circumstances unique to you and your loss, you may find that the content of this book and/or the process of journaling your responses may prove too overwhelming.

First, feelings of shock, disbelief, and numbness are characteristic of early grief. The stronger your attachment to the person who died,

WHEN YOUR SOULMATE DIES

the longer your period of shock and numbness is likely to be. If you are still feeling acute shock over the death, you might want to set this book aside for the time being. You will probably find it more helpful six months to a year from now.

Similarly, if you are finding it extremely challenging to function in your day-to-day life, I would ask you to consider seeking the support of a compassionate grief counselor as you simultaneously engage with this book. Again, this does not mean something is "wrong" with you. On the contrary, it means that your loss was so devastating that it would overwhelm anyone's capacity to cope. If a grief counselor isn't right for you, then a grief support group might be. Or, you might find that the ongoing, reliable companionship of a friend who is a good listener is just the support you need as you work through this book and your grief.

Thank you for entrusting me to guide this exploration. Stories of love and loss are the most precious in the universe—those capturing soulmates especially so. As you read this book and share your unique story, please know that I am honored to facilitate and bear witness to your work of mourning. It may be the most important work you have ever done.

Bless you. I hope we meet one day.

Alan D. Wolfelt

Date:

Do you feel ready to read and write in this book? Why or why not?

Please write about the who, why, when, and how of your soulmate's death.

Who:

Why:

When:

How:

You are invited to tape or glue a photo of your soulmate here and share a little about when and where the photo was taken.

In what ways was your relationship a soulmate relationship?

Please write about whether you knew instantly you were soulmates or you became soulmates over time.

What are your beliefs about the soul?

Do you believe you were connected at the soul level to this person? If so, how? Do you also believe your souls will continue to be connected after death? What are your beliefs or doubts about this?

How does (or doesn't) the idea of two halves joining to become one suit the relationship you had with your soulmate?

In what ways has your grief since your soulmate's death been different than other griefs you have experienced in your life?

What does your grief (thoughts and feelings on the inside) consist of today?

Which mourning (expressing thoughts and feelings outside yourself) behaviors, activities, or practices have you engaged in since your soulmate's death?

If you could tell your soulmate one thing right now, what would it be?

CHAPTER ONE

SOULMATE LOVE

"A soulmate is someone to whom we feel profoundly connected, as though the communicating and communing that take place between us were not the product of intentional efforts, but rather a divine grace."

— Thomas Moore

Love and grief are two sides of the same precious coin. One does not—and cannot—exist without the other. They are the yin and yang of our lives. Because human beings die, for those of us who continue to live there is no such thing as love without also, eventually, loss.

After a death, the stronger the love that bound two people who are now separated, the stronger the grief in the survivor. As we began to consider in this book's Introduction, soulmate love is an especially profound kind of love and connection. I am not someone who generally believes it is helpful to rank or compare loves and their subsequent grief, but I will say that in all my many years as a grief counselor and educator, the people who came to me for help with some of the most devastating, overwhelming feelings of grief and loss were grieving parents and grieving soulmates.

But before we begin to consider how to cope with your overwhelming grief, I would first like to back up and talk some more about the love that characterizes soulmate relationships. Love is what makes life meaningful. Deep love seems to make life deeply meaningful for soulmates. But *how* is soulmate love so strong and deep? In this chapter we'll review some of the most common characteristics of the soulmate relationship, which, when combined, form such a potent bond. As you'll see in later chapters, this review will be essential to our understanding of the flipside of soulmate love: soulmate grief.

Along the way, I'll invite you to write a little about your own singular

soulmate experience with each of the characteristics. Remember—
there are no rights and wrongs here. Your soulmate relationship
may not have featured all of these characteristics. In addition, other
attributes that you felt were central to your relationship may not
be listed. The uniqueness of your special relationship could never
be fully captured in a few pages, anyway. You know that, and I
know that. Rather than being an exhaustive or definitive list, the
characteristics that follow—presented in no particular order—
were simply those that most stood out to me in my work and
communications with grieving soulmates.

Shared values

The soulmate relationship is typically built on a bedrock of shared
values and beliefs. Without this foundation, a soulmate relationship
may not be possible.

*"We iteratively sought
out and agreed upon
fundamental truths in
raising our family. When
a crossroads came,
we prayed and sought
counsel about which
path to take. Our prayer
life together matured as
we aged."*

— Bob Troublefield

Following are some of the most
common shared values I was able to
glean from the many letters I received
from grieving soulmates:

- Our family is our priority.
- Our faith and/or religion and/or
  spirituality is essential.
- We value spending time together
  with friends.
- We value volunteerism and giving
  back.
- We value sharing fun experiences.
- We value creating and maintaining a comfortable home.

Are there others you would add?

Of course, each soulmate pair has its own unique set of values
and beliefs. It doesn't matter precisely what the values and beliefs

consist of. What matters is that the partners generally agree on the important stuff. They are on the same Page with a capital P. Believing in and living the same principles seems to open the door to the other soulmate characteristics that follow.

I look to the idea of "soul" again when I consider this attribute of the soulmate relationship. Perhaps the soul comes down to earth with a profound knowing of the most important truths of existence. Maybe souls that join together as soulmates for their tenure as human beings are souls that somehow escaped the snare of the earthly ego and never lost this knowing.

Which significant values and beliefs did you and your soulmate share? Were there any you didn't hold in common? How did your shared or unshared values affect your relationship?

Best friends

Whether they are also lovers or not, soulmates almost always describe themselves as best friends. They genuinely like each other. They communicate. They talk regularly and share things big and small. They confide in one another. They are loyal to one another. They make joint decisions. They go through life's ups and downs together as if on a bicycle built for two.

Trust, in turn, is what lies beneath the best-friends nature of the soulmate relationship. Soulmates tend to trust one another more than they trust anyone else. They are honest with one another. They "show up" for one another, day in and day out. When one of them makes a mistake, they tend to forgive. And because of this earned and demonstrated mutual trust, they feel safe and secure in their relationship and thus in life.

"He was my safe place. When Darren was there, I knew I was cared for, and I had this undeniable confidence that all was as it should be."

— Megan Quinn

Some soulmates describe this sense of safety in the soulmate relationship as feeling "at home." Others describe a sense of peace. "When I was with him, I felt peacefulness never before experienced," wrote Marcia Teachout. Geralyn Nathe-Evans concurred, saying that she and her husband felt they had arrived at "a place of great peace and calm, love and devotion."

When a soulmate dies, chaos replaces peace and calm. Trust is obliterated. And the surviving soulmate is suddenly without his or her best friend. No wonder the grief is so devastating.

Were you and your soulmate best friends? If yes, in what ways? If not, why not? How important was trust to your relationship? Did you experience a feeling of being "at home" or "at peace" with your soulmate? If so, how?

Companionship

Soulmates usually spend lots of time together. They tend to be inseparable companions. Their love is not only deep, it is daily. Most soulmates live in the same household, and their lives revolve around one another. They enjoy sharing the rituals of their daily lives, and even when they part for separate activities—for work or for individual hobbies, for example—they tend to keep tabs on one another throughout the day with phone calls or texting. Upon returning home they may spend some time catching up with one another, taking turns giving reports on their time apart. In fact, the soulmate relationship is typically an everyday kind of relationship built on what may seem from the outside like the most mundane details.

> *"We were two peas-in-a-pod, and we could even read each other's minds. We both worked full-time jobs but spent all of our non-work hours together. We would grocery shop together, clean house together, work in the yard together, and perform volunteer work together. We were not only husband and wife but best friends, lovers, confidants, caregivers, and soulmates."*
>
> — Jo Anne Gregory

I said it before and I'll say it again: the deeper the love, the deeper the grief after a death. I would also add: the more present the love in life, the more present the grief after death. A relationship built on near-constant companionship can't help but leave the surviving person in a deep void when one soulmate dies. The surviving soulmate is confronted with the physical reality of the loss nearly constantly.

When you have grown accustomed to orbiting every day around someone whose company you enjoy and have grown to depend on—and suddenly that person is gone—your minute-by-minute existence is thrown into disarray. You have not only lost your best friend and confidant, you may also have lost your breakfast companion, your laundry partner, your sous chef, your walking buddy, your TV-watching sidekick, and your bedwarmer in one fell swoop—and this is to mention just a few of the myriad facets of daily presence you may now be missing.

What did your day-to-day companionship with your soulmate consist of, especially in the last years of your relationship?

Intimacy and attraction

The joy of physical contact with others is something we revel in when we are young children but tend to lose as we grow older. In our culture, rarely do adults hug and touch one another on a daily basis—but soulmates often do. They are among the privileged few who continue to enjoy the grounding and healing benefits of regular physical contact.

"We held hands whenever we could—walking, in the car, at the store, and at church. There is something about skin-to-skin contact with your best friend."

— Rita Roush

"We didn't care that we showed people how much we loved each other, whether by holding hands, giving a kiss, or just looking at each other as if no one else existed but us two."

— Marsha Pettigrew

"Tall, dark, handsome, but humble and shy, Ron asked me to dance back in 1969. Magnetism. Attraction. I said yes."

— Marilyn Stroud

Soulmates who are also lovers share the intimacy of sexuality as well as general physical closeness, both of which enhance their bond. They are comfortable with one another's bodies as well as personalities, likes and dislikes, and other aspects of self. Some soulmates described the spark of physical passion as being central to their relationships, while others spoke of their long-term intimacy as more of a product of trust, commitment, communication, and spiritual connection.

Please describe the attraction, passion, and intimacy you and your soulmate shared. In what ways did your physical closeness change throughout the course of your relationship?

Sense of humor

Soulmates often share a similar sense of humor, or, if they do not, an appreciation for one another's sense of humor. A sense of fun, levity,

> *"He had a wonderful gift of gab and humor. Many of our days together began with a laugh. He was, in countless ways, my North Star."*
>
> — Laura Renker

and laughter is typically central to the soulmate relationship. "Every day we spent together we made a fun day, regardless of whether we were doing nothing or doing something," wrote Karen Steen. Patti Stahl said that her soulmate brother was the funniest man she knew. "You know when you just feel better being around certain people…just because? That was how I felt with Mike." And Ruth Turner wrote, "He made me laugh, and that is such a joy that I miss now with him gone."

As Ruth shared, laughter is one of life's greatest joys, and so to spend your days in companionship with someone who loves to laugh, make you laugh, and just have fun is a gift of the highest order. To have that gift taken away must then also be a loss of the highest order.

Write about your soulmate's sense of humor and desire to have fun in life and how those intersected with or amplified your own.

Vulnerability

Soulmates open themselves to one another. Seeing the awesome possibilities enabled by the trust we discussed above, they let down their guards and allow their partners to see them as they are, in all their glory *and* all their faults. Any initial insecurities, vanity, or posturing they may have brought to the relationship are usually dropped over time. The ego, which worries about false things like appearances, status, and being right, fades into the background, and the soul, which is concerned with truths such as the timeless spirit, the beauty of existence, joy, and love, comes to the fore.

"We hurt together when one hurt and put each other's needs above our own. We laughed uncontrollably together and cried out loud together. We lived life together, heart to heart."

— Bob Troublefield

Research professor and author Brené Brown says that we "cultivate love when we allow our most vulnerable and powerful selves to be seen and known." From inside the context of the soulmate relationship, we are able to see that vulnerability is not the weakness we may have thought of it as but rather the asset that brings soulmates closer and closer together, creating the conditions for their love to continually deepen. The more vulnerable they allow themselves to be with one another, the tighter their bond.

Alas, it is this same vulnerability that opens soulmates to such profound grief...but also, as we will soon discuss, to such profound hope and healing.

In what ways did you and your soulmate open yourselves to one another? How did your mutual vulnerability enhance and grow your relationship?

Kindness

Plain old kindness may actually be a superpower when it comes to soulmate relationships. Don't get me wrong—soulmates are not *always* nice to one another. As human beings, they are not perfect.

> *"A true soulmate is probably the most important person you will ever meet, because they tear down your walls and shake you awake."*
>
> — Elizabeth Gilbert

They don't always agree, and they may be unkind to one another sometimes. Yet most of the time soulmates make the effort to treat each other with courtesy and kindness.

What kindness looks like varies from relationship to relationship, of course. One soulmate may be good at thoughtful conversation, while another may be good at expressing care by completing essential household tasks or simply being present and attentive. Physical kindness may involve hugs and kisses; social kindness could include helping a less socially skilled partner navigate gatherings and events. While it comes in many forms, genuine soulmate kindness requires mutual respect and empathy.

When a thousand daily kindnesses are suddenly revoked by death, what happens? The surviving soulmate is no longer attended to and cared for in the same way. It can leave you feeling like the sun got turned off—cold and lost in the dark.

How were you and your soulmate kind to one another? Did your kindness evolve over the years? If so, in what ways?

Longevity

Many (but sadly, not all) soulmates are fortunate to share decades together. For some it will be the longest close relationship of their lives. In fact, a number of the soulmates who wrote to me spoke of meeting as teenagers. The longevity of their relationship hones and enhances their closeness.

"We had an enviable marriage in the later years, an easy companionship centered on love, commitment, and putting each other first. Our relationship hadn't always been that way, which was why it was all the more incredible in its richness."

— Mary Potter Kenyon

In fact, many soulmates seem to get closer and closer as they grow older together. Quite a few soulmates have told me that their years and experiences together are what allowed them to transform into soulmates. They seem to find a "together rhythm," especially, for those who are also parents, after their children have grown and left home.

How long were you in a relationship with your soulmate? Did the relationship deepen over time? Why or why not? How would you say the duration of your relationship has affected your grief?

▢ *Perseverance*

Coupled with longevity is the quality of perseverance. Grieving soulmate stories almost always include some variation on this phrase: "We've been through so much together." Soulmates are often partners who learn to weather adversity as a team. Life is replete with loss, and soulmates join to hold each other up and persevere in the face of challenges such as illness, job loss, financial straits, aging, legal troubles, relocation, crises of faith, childrearing, and, of course, the death of loved ones.

While naturally the soulmate stories I've been privileged to hear include times of shared joy as well, I've noticed they tend to focus even more on times of shared loss. That's because our griefs not only test us, they reveal us. They strip away everything inconsequential, leaving us exposed and shattered. When two people allow themselves to be completely vulnerable to one another at such times, transparent and genuine, their souls meet. Mustering the fortitude to offer each other kindness, attention, and assistance when times are tough strengthens the soulmate bond more mightily than exclusively enjoying good times together can.

Write about the most significant losses you and your soulmate experienced during the course of your relationship. How did you survive them together?

Selflessness and sacrifice

Soulmates try to put their relationship needs above their own individual needs. While they do not lose their individuality to the relationship, they tend to subordinate personal desires that may conflict with the shared goals of the relationship. They compromise and sacrifice, but they do so in the hopes that their investment will pay off a hundredfold in the form of shared joy and meaning.

Soulmates put their partner's needs above their own individual needs as well sometimes. Do you remember "The Gift of the Magi," by O. Henry? In the story Christmas is approaching, and the young married couple is too poor to be able to give each other gifts. So, unbeknownst to one another, the wife sells her beautiful hair to buy the husband a platinum pocket-watch chain, and the husband sells his pocket watch to buy the wife a set of decorative hair combs. They end up realizing, of course, that their mutual, selfless love is the greatest gift of all.

Selflessness and sacrifice are part of many types of relationships, but what seems to make this quality unique in the soulmate relationship is the approximate equality in the degrees of selflessness and sacrifice. While the contributions each makes to the relationship are different, it is understood that both partners sacrifice and give of themselves more or less equally.

In which ways did each of you exhibit selflessness and sacrifice in your soulmate relationship? Were your sacrifices more or less equal? How so or how not?

Adventure

We've talked about soulmates' perseverance through adversity; this is a corollary to that—a sense of life as an adventure that is more meaningful when shared.

Not all soulmates are adventurers in the risk-taking, traveler sense of the word. Sure, some couples literally climb mountains, sail seas, and explore foreign lands. Those who do definitely express their mutual passion for life through physical and geographical exploits. Yet soulmates whose sense of adventure runs more to the everyday often feel just as united in their passion for life.

Soulmates often try new things together. They make room for each other to grow and change. They revel in the day ahead and big and small adventures to come. They also tend to enjoy reminiscing together about shared past adventures.

Soulmates seem to look at life this way: We don't know what's going to happen next, but whatever it is, we will face it head on with as much honesty and joy as possible—together.

For my soulmate and me, adventure was about...

Rituals

Soulmates typically share and enjoy many day-to-day activities. What to non-soulmates may feel like neutral or even boring tasks—such as morning coffee or a daily walk—to soulmates may feel like sacred rituals. They can imbue even the most mundane routines with a sense of specialness and privilege (more on that next). Their capacity for presence elevates the everyday to the exceptional, and the exceptional to the extraordinary.

"When walking around our 'back forty' after dinner nightly through the 41 years, we held hands. We felt the magnetism, the draw."

— Marilyn Stroud

All of us turn to ritual when we want to acknowledge and celebrate a special occasion. That's why things like birthday cakes and candles, weddings, and funerals are so important. At these times, everyday words and actions aren't powerful enough to express our most profound feelings, but ritual is. Soulmates intuit the power of ritual and tend to harness it more often to express and honor their special love.

Which daily and weekly rituals did you and your soulmate share? What about less frequent, bigger rituals, such as anniversary events?

☐ *A sense of privilege and honor*

Soulmates seem to appreciate their good fortune. They move through life together aware that not all relationships enjoy the attributes we've been talking about in this chapter. Rather than feeling smug, however, they feel lucky.

Joanne Churilla wrote to me about the death of her soulmate, John, whom she didn't meet until she was 50 and he 67. She was divorced, as was he. "We were two wounded birds trying to learn to fly again," she said. "During the 20 years we had together, we certainly did learn to fly again as partners in love with life and grateful for finding each other."

Joanne's feeling of gratitude pervaded most of the letters I received from grieving soulmates. While they were and still are devastated by their losses, they feel so grateful for the relationship they were privileged to be a part of.

The concepts of privilege and gratitude are related closely to honoring. If you feel grateful for something, you honor it. You regard it with great respect. You hold it in high esteem. Soulmates hold each other in high esteem. They regard each other with respect. They honor one another in life, and the survivor continues to honor the partner who died after his or her death:

"The soul urges me to remember and honor the special relationship and love my husband and I shared," wrote Allison Wysota.

"I realized I need to honor my friend in ways that she demonstrated were important to her," wrote Sharon Triano-Kott.

"I struggle at times, but what gets me through is the respect and admiration for my courageous mother; I will always honor her," wrote Michele Hackett.

Like many of the characteristics we've been reviewing in this chapter, I believe that a sense of privilege as well as the capacity to be grateful and honor are learned skills. Soulmates seem to tend to get better at them together over time. The fact that they are learnable will be important in our discussions to come.

When your soulmate was alive, in what ways did you feel privileged or lucky to have such a relationship? How did you honor your soulmate during your relationship? In what ways did your soulmate honor you during your relationship? In what ways are you honoring him or her since the death?

THE LOVE OF YOUR LIFE

The characteristics we've reviewed in this chapter seem to be the main ingredients that are essential to creating the depth of the bond that defines a soulmate relationship. If we reduced this recipe to shorthand, it might look something like this:

Shared values + best friends + companionship + physical closeness + intimacy + sense of humor + vulnerability + kindness + longevity + perseverance + selflessness + adventure + rituals + a sense of privilege and honor = The love of your life

Of course, not every soulmate relationship will fit this exact formula, and as I've said, we are not here to determine which relationships would pass some silly soulmate test. (We'll leave such nonsense to Facebook.) But examining the characteristics of the soulmate relationship, it turns out, is a helpful step on the way to figuring out how to authentically mourn and heal after the love of your life dies. That's what we'll be covering next.

> *"I was a widower at the age of 52, with three children, but I was fortunate to have a successful, loving marriage to my best friend. Not everyone gets that in life."*
>
> — Don Mueller

Were other characteristics not mentioned in this chapter important in your relationship with your soulmate? If so, I invite you to write about them here.

CHAPTER TWO
HEROIC MOURNING

"I always knew he was my hero, but when I witnessed how he handled this disease, I fell in love with him all over again."

— Janet Tompkins

This book promises to be a "guide to healing through heroic mourning." In the Introduction we talked a little about what mourning is—the outward expression of our inward grief. For anyone who is experiencing any kind of significant grief, mourning is the way to healing. It is essential not only to getting through the pain but eventually to finding a path to continuing on with a life of meaning and purpose.

But "heroic" mourning? What does *that* mean?

When I first began thinking about this resource, I realized it would have to offer something *more*. As I explained in the Preface, I had already written a book for those grieving the death of a spouse. In addition to *Healing a Spouse's Grieving Heart*, my *100 Ideas* series also already included specialized books for grieving parents, grieving adult children, and other unique relationship losses and causes of death. Even so, in my travels across the country and around the world to speak about the normal and necessary process of grief, I continued to meet grieving soulmates who felt their special needs were not yet being adequately addressed in my writings.

"Please write a book for those of us who are struggling with the death of a soulmate," they would say to me. "Our grief is uniquely devastating. We need your help."

And so I thought about it, and I talked to grieving soulmates, and I thought about it some more. Years passed. In the meantime, I wrote a number of other books, one of which focused on love and grief

(*Loving from the Outside In, Mourning from the Inside Out*), which helped me begin to more deeply consider soulmate relationships. A number of months ago I also solicited stories from grieving soulmates, so I could ensure their authentic voices were heard, their stories told, and their wise counsel passed along.

Through all of these efforts to understand the unique needs of soulmate grief, I noticed a striking pattern. Soulmate stories, I realized, unlike most stories of love and loss, tended to include certain words that we don't often use in ordinary conversation— words like:

HERO
LOYALTY SACRIFICE
RITUALS FATE ETERNITY
HONOR FATE OATH
SOUL VOW ADVENTURE
COMMITMENT
FAITH

These words are lofty. They are concerned with the biggest Ideas in life. And they reminded me of something… What was it?

Eventually I realized that the language soulmates often used to tell their stories conjured, for me, medieval knights, quests, and courtly love. They evoked dangers and heroes, courage and honor, championing the good and upholding the right. There was a mythic and grand quality to their tales of love and death. No wonder the struggles of their grief felt equally epic.

As I've said, the stronger the attachment in life, the stronger the resulting grief when the attachment is broken. The grand language soulmates use to describe their relationships tells me that

> *"Many people said to me, 'But you knew he was sick; why are you so shocked at his death now?' Those words cut like a knife. I just somehow thought our love could conquer all! When he left my physical world, a part a me went with him. The emptiness is devastating."*
>
> — Karen Steen

soulmate love is larger than life. The consequence is that soulmate grief is also larger than life.

Which brings me to the real question of this book: How do you heal such legendary grief?

And the answer is: You mourn as you loved—grandly and deeply. You mourn heroically.

Soulmate grief is effectively mourned by relying on all the learned characteristics and skills we talked about in the last chapter. They served you well in love, and if you actively engage with them now, they will also serve you well in grief.

In what ways was your soulmate relationship characterized by love that was grand or larger than life?

HEROIC MOURNING

Let me begin this section by saying that I believe all mourning is heroic. Grief is always deeply challenging and painful. And especially in our grief-avoidant culture, it takes courage and fortitude for anyone to openly engage with and express their grief for as long as it takes. We're taught to "hold it together," "keep our chins up," and "move on," when what we really need to do is let it fall apart, let the tears run freely down our chins, and stay right where we are for as long as we need to. To create a category called "heroic mourning" is in no way to denigrate or diminish more typical mourning. I think of them more as siblings than as greater than and less than.

Yet if soulmate relationships are based on an epic love, then I humbly suggest that soulmate mourning needs to be equally epic. To effectively reconcile your outsized grief, your mourning must be Heroic with a capital H. I have come to believe that it takes medieval-style bravery. It may also require larger-than-life levels of faith, sacrifice, loyalty, commitment, adventure, and honor.

It has come to pass that the love of your life has unleashed the grief of your life. Now you must muster the courage to mourn as well and as deeply as you loved.

Here's how I feel about this idea of heroic mourning and the potential need for me to mourn more deeply than I have ever mourned before:

WHEN YOUR SOULMATE DIES

WHAT HEROIC MOURNING IS NOT

When I solicited loss stories from grieving soulmates in preparation for this book, I received one letter from a woman who seemed to feel insulted by the term "heroic mourning."

"There's nothing heroic about the mourning process," she wrote. "It's tough and it's hardscrabble. Does heroic mean you exist by performing the familiar tasks you know just to stay alive? Is it heroic to not shed the tears that come unexpectedly? Can you mourn heroically when you've lost your spark, your reason for being, your real pleasure in living?"

I understand that the idea of heroic mourning could be interpreted, at first glance, as ridiculous and even disrespectful. Like this woman, as a grieving soulmate you are devastated. You are torn apart. You are deeply injured— metaphorically if not literally laid low and curled into a ball on the floor. How is your suffering heroic? How can you be asked to be the hero when you're the one who clearly needs saving?

I hope to answer these crucial questions in the chapters ahead. In the meantime, I ask you to continue on with an open mind. Rest assured that the concept of heroic mourning honors all of your natural and necessary feelings of grief. It respects you as the expert of your own journey. It does not ask you to "overcome" or deny your feelings but rather to ever so slowly learn to listen to and befriend them. It would never suggest that you not cry. Tears of grief are sacred. And always, always it empathizes with your larger-than-life pain and need for normal reactions like despair, anger, and withdrawal. It recognizes that encountering these is heroic in its own right.

Heroic mourning is not maintaining a stiff upper lip. Neither is it is just learning to get by. Instead, it is being humbled by your grief. It is surrendering to it. It is embracing your grief as well as using the lessons you learned throughout your soulmate love story to mourn well. If you can muster the heroic courage it takes to meet your outsized mourning needs, you will not only survive, you will learn to thrive again.

No, your life will never be the same, but it can once again be meaningful. And only heroic mourning can get you there.

GRIEF AS A QUEST

I often talk about grief as a journey through the wilderness. It is dangerous and lonely. It can be cold and dark. Grievers often feel lost there for a long, long time. You probably recognize this metaphor of the wilderness of grief. Since your soulmate died, I imagine you, too, have often felt afraid, cold, lonely, and lost in the dark.

From here on out, I am challenging you, as a heroic mourner, to consider your grief journey as a quest. You are still in the wilderness of your grief, and you may well still be lost. But because you are now taking on the responsibility of a quest, you will begin to think of your journey as a long, arduous search for something. You have a goal. And like the knights of old, you have a noble reason for achieving your goal—a reason that is bigger than you or any other individual person.

Your goal on this quest is no less than to reconcile your epic grief and find meaning again in your continued living. It will not be easy. Your grief is profoundly wide and deep. You already know that it is complicated. It is much more challenging than most if not all other griefs you have experienced in your life thus far. But I believe you are capable of encountering and moving through all the dangers along the way. I have faith that you have within you the strength to achieve your goal.

I don't know you. So how can I have such blind faith in someone I've never met? And why am I so sure that you, too, should be certain in your capacity to mourn well and go on to live well again?

Here's how I know: I've been privileged to bear witness to the healing of many grieving soulmates in my decades as a grief counselor and educator, but more important, I am giving you soulmate credit. You weren't just half of a soulmate relationship. You were and are a soulmate. During the course of your relationship, you learned how to embody many or all of the characteristics we reviewed in the last chapter.

Because you are a soulmate, you get which values really matter in life. You know how to cultivate friendship. You excel at companionship. You are well acquainted with the power of physical connection. You appreciate the joy of laughter. You know how to be vulnerable and have witnessed the transformative things that can happen when you open yourself to vulnerability. You're good at kindness. You know how to see things through over the long haul. You persevere like nobody's business. You're a master at selflessness and sacrifice. You think of life as an adventure. You have borne witness to the power of rituals. And despite your loss, you understand what a privilege and honor it was to have experienced a soulmate relationship. You appreciate the gift of gratitude.

I am so sure that you have the capacity to succeed at your grief quest because the skills it will take are the same skills you mastered as a soulmate.

How do you feel about embarking on a quest to reconcile your epic grief and find meaning again in your continued life?

COMMITTING TO YOUR QUEST

Before you embark on your quest, you must commit to it. You must set your intention to embrace and eventually reconcile your larger-than-life grief. Notice how Mary tells us in the quote at left that she had to make a conscious choice to mourn her pain and find meaning again. It didn't just happen.

"I mined the pain, using it to write and speak on grief, and reaching out to others who are hurting. I became a better person for having known such a beautiful man. This was a conscious choice, and one I know David would be proud of."

— Mary Potter Kenyon

This puts you at a crossroads. You too have a choice. You can choose, as Mary did, to do the admittedly arduous and painful work of fully encountering and expressing your soulmate grief so that you can learn to find meaning in life again. Or you can choose to live a shadow-life for the remainder of your days, grieving deeply inside but not mourning heroically, and never really, truly, and fully engaging with life again.

Both hurt. Neither is fair. Neither is your most fervent wish, which would be to have your soulmate alive and well again. One involves more gumption, risk-taking, and effort. One involves more aloneness, and, ultimately, despair.

"I started one-on-one counseling sessions since I still had trouble speaking and just cried continuously. My counselor recommended journaling. What I couldn't speak, I could express in written form."

— Charles Stackhouse

Essentially, you are at a fork in the road: one way leads to anxiety, the other to depression. I agree—neither seems like a good choice.

I'm encouraging you to take the path of mourning. To encounter and deeply embrace your grief. That's terrifying. As C.S. Lewis noted, "No one ever told me that grief felt so like fear." And what causes anxiety? Fear. Heroic mourning means mustering the courage to face the fear. Grieving soulmate Barbara Mogel chose this path. "To honor my husband, a firefighter for nearly 25 years," she wrote to me, "I decided that in my grief I would do as he did: run toward my fears."

Your other option is depression. You can choose to avoid and deny your grief as much as possible. When denial and avoidance aren't sufficient—because your grief is powerful, it will keep trying to get your attention—you can choose to repress. You can keep your grief locked inside and suffer in silence. Trouble is, denial, avoidance, and repression lead to depression. On this path, you spend the rest of your life living in the shadow of the ghosts of grief. You die while you are alive.

Which path will you choose?

I hope with all of my heart you will pick the first path. I know you have what it takes. After all, you chose the path of the soulmate before, despite the fact that it involved more risk and higher ups and downs than a life alone. Even though it wasn't always easy, you chose to connect rather than isolate. You chose to risk rather than protect.

Was the path of the soulmate worth it, even though it ended in overwhelming grief? Of course, most of you will say. I promise you now that the path of the soulmate who chooses to heroically mourn is also worth it.

I appreciate, though, that not everyone who is reading this book is ready to commit to this quest. Especially if you are still in the shock-and-numbness-filled early weeks and months of your grief, you may want to set this book aside for a time and return to it later. Likewise, if the challenge of this quest fills you with indignation, anger, or despair, you may not be ready. And remember our earlier conversation about complicated grief? Because soulmate grief is naturally complicated, you may also need the support of a good grief counselor and/or support group before you begin this quest.

One last thought about your choice to commit to this quest or not: What would your soulmate want for you? Which choice better honors them and the relationship you shared? If you believe in soulmates, you may well also believe that their souls are watching you now. They know you are worthy, as do I.

Are you ready to commit to this quest? Why or why not?

Which path would your soulmate want you to choose? Why?

If and when you are ready, please make your commitment on paper here. To provide you with even more divine momentum, consider having a good friend or responsibility partner witness it below.

MY GRIEF QUEST COMMITMENT

On this the _____ day of _____, 20_____,

I, _____, soulmate of_____,

who died on the _____ day of _____,

20_____, do hereby swear to, slowly and over time, fully embrace

my natural, necessary, and larger-than-life grief and openly and

actively find ways to heroically mourn. My vow is to continually

move toward and ultimately reconcile my profound soulmate grief

so that I can find meaning in my continued living. To this quest I

pledge my courage, loyalty, mercy, honesty, humility, perseverance,

and love.

_____

Your signature

_____

Witness

CHAPTER THREE

AN INTRODUCTION TO

THE SIX NEEDS OF HEROIC MOURNING

"I might not have wanted to adapt. I might have been resistant to the idea of a new life. I might have continued to say, 'But I don't want to live without him.' But there is a quiet voice in my head trying to help me heal on a daily basis, and that is my soul. And it is still very much connected to my husband, Adam. The soul gently guides and encourages me so I can make progress towards engaging in this life again. The soul continually reminds me that my connection to my husband, our love, remains intact and steadfast. The soul urges me to remember and honor the special relationship and love my husband and I shared, the one I am so grateful to have had."

— Allison Wysota

When someone we love dies, our hearts and minds are drowning in grief. Inside, we can't help but feel all kinds of feelings—potentially ranging from shock and numbness to confusion, anxiety, anger, guilt, relief, and, of course, sadness and depression, as well as others. We can't help but think all kinds of thoughts.

But no matter what's going on inside our hearts and minds, it's only through active, outward mourning that we begin to heal. This is how we start to integrate our grief and give it momentum. You see, over time, grief-in-motion evolves. It begins to soften. It starts to heal. It never completely goes away, but like a healed wound, it becomes part of the imperfect wholeness of who we are.

Grief is the vehicle; mourning is the engine.
Grief is the paint; mourning is the act of painting.
Grief is the rock; mourning is the catapult.
Grief is the noun; mourning is the verb.

I've proposed that because your soulmate grief is larger than life, it will take larger-than-life mourning to move it toward reconciliation. It will take what I'm calling heroic mourning.

Your heroic mourning quest will be your own unique journey, with many particular twists and turns. Along the way, I want you to remember that there are no rights or wrongs, really. Your quest will take as long as it takes. It will switchback and repeat and dead end as much as it needs to. As long as you remain committed to actively expressing your grief, being gentle and patient with yourself and stopping for rest and withdrawal as often as you need to, you can trust that you are doing the work you need to do.

Still, it's easy to feel lost in grief. Even if you are actively mourning, engaging with your grief often and openly, you may find yourself floundering. How can you really tell if things are getting better? What if you're not mourning effectively? Are you really and truly on the right path?

Fortunately, there are six major waystations to be on the watch for on your quest. I call them the needs of mourning, and they apply to all kinds of grief. They are

HEROIC MOURNING NEED 1: Acknowledge the reality of your soulmate's death

HEROIC MOURNING NEED 2: Embrace the pain of the loss

HEROIC MOURNING NEED 3: Remember your soulmate

HEROIC MOURNING NEED 4: Develop a new self-identity

HEROIC MOURNING NEED 5: Search for meaning

HEROIC MOURNING NEED 6: Receive ongoing support from others

All grievers must meet these needs of mourning in order to heal after a significant loss, but for soulmates, as we have discussed, the needs have been made more complicated by the unusually close nature of the relationship. So while all grievers have to confront the six needs of mourning, the needs become outsized for soulmates. For you, they are the needs of heroic mourning. In the following chapters, we'll be taking a closer look at needs, one at a time, as they relate to your unique grief journey and the characteristics of the soulmate relationship we reviewed in Chapter One.

Another thing I want you to keep in mind as you move forward in this book is that though the needs of mourning are numbered 1 through 6, mourning is never an orderly progression toward healing. As you have probably already learned, your quest toward reconciliation will not always be predictable or forward-moving. It is not uncommon for grief to be a one-step-forward, two-steps-back kind of process. In fact, grief often gets worse before it gets better.

What's more, you may have heard of the "stages" of grief, first proposed in 1969 by Elisabeth Kübler-Ross's landmark text, *On Death and Dying.* In this book she lists the five stages of grief that she saw terminally ill patients experience in the face of their own impending deaths: denial, anger, bargaining, depression, and acceptance. However, she never intended for her five stages to be applied to all grief or to be interpreted as a rigid, linear sequence to be followed by all mourners. Besides, the stages of grief concept is mostly about what you think and feel inside. Our focus in the remainder of this book is what to *do* about what you think and feel inside—in other words, how to actively mourn.

Since your soulmate died, have you been both grieving and mourning? Please write about what your internal grief is like as well as your efforts at external mourning.

In what ways have you already begun to encounter the six needs of mourning?

PREPARING FOR YOUR QUEST

Now that we've reviewed the fundamentals of soulmate grief and the basic concepts of heroic mourning, it's almost time to embark. There's just one more topic I want to cover before we venture into the more specific, how-to suggestions of heroically mourning your soulmate grief—and that is the rules of the road.

As a grieving soulmate who has vowed to mourn heroically on a quest to reconcile your grief and find meaning again in your continued living, I am also asking you to promise to agree to live by a code of honor. This code of honor, though, is not about chivalry and pomp and circumstance. Instead, it's about honoring yourself and your day-to-day survival needs along the way.

Your quest to heal your grief is a challenge—possibly the biggest challenge of your life so far. And to meet this challenge, you will have to take good care of yourself. Here are the promises I hope you will make:

THE GRIEVING SOULMATE'S CODE OF HONOR

1. I will remember that only I can be the master of my quest. Only I can tell what is right and what is wrong for me.

2. I will dose myself with my grief and mourning, embracing and engaging with it a bit at a time and then retreating again when I am spent.

3. I will be patient with myself. Whenever I feel frustrated, I will remind myself that there is no timetable, and there are no rewards for speed.

4. I will be gentle with myself. I have been grievously wounded. I need and deserve gentle, loving, compassionate care from myself as well as from others.

5. I will take care of myself physically. When I am feeling tired, I will rest. I will eat foods that help my body run well and feel good; I will drink ample water; I will move my body regularly by taking walks or other exercise I enjoy.

6. I will take care of myself cognitively. I will not overtax my mind when I feel overwhelmed. I will engage in cognitive tasks that give me energy, entertainment, or solace.

7. I will take care of myself emotionally. My emotions are tender. They require tender loving care.

8. I will take care of myself socially. My friends and family may withdraw because they don't know how to help me. Others may judge or try to direct my grief. I will seek out the company of those who can listen and be present to my mourning without feeling the need to take it away.

9. I will take care of myself spiritually. If spirituality is part of my life, I will express it as I see fit.

10. I will see a grief counselor, support group, and/or physician if I am having trouble functioning day-to-day because of my naturally complicated grief. I will also turn to them if I get stuck, am considering harming myself or someone else, or just want a little extra support. Reaching out for help of this kind is not weak; it is strong and heroic.

This Code of Honor, when combined with the Quest Commitment you completed on page 56 and the soulmate strengths we reviewed in Chapter One, synergize to create a powerful force for healing. Together, they are the force that will ensure that you not only survive your profound grief but eventually achieve a new wholeheartedness.

Now let's take a closer look at the needs of heroic mourning, one by one, and ideas for meeting each of them. We'll also hear from other grieving soulmates about what has worked for them.

How have you been doing so far with the principles of the Grieving Soulmate's Code of Honor? Which are you naturally better at and which are naturally harder for you? Are there any you disagree with? If so, why?

CHAPTER FOUR

HEROIC MOURNING NEED 1.

ACKNOWLEDGE THE REALITY OF YOUR SOULMATE'S DEATH

"I did everything I could to convince myself that his death was a nightmare. Although my brain knew he was gone, my heart did not."

— Julie Lynn McIntyre

This first need of heroic mourning involves gently yet, over time, thoroughly confronting the reality that your soulmate will never physically be present in your life again. Death is always a hard reality to come to terms with, but for soulmates, it can seem shockingly surreal and counterintuitive. After all, your relationship was so much about living and enjoying each present moment of life together.

> *"I had to tell my brain a hundred times a day that Lee was really gone, hoping (or perhaps dreading) the reality would sink in."*
>
> — Debra Milligan

Common thoughts and feelings for soulmates encountering this need of mourning include numbness, shock, disbelief, denial, disorganization, and confusion. You may find yourself experiencing these feelings much more deeply and for a much longer period of time than you did after other losses in your life. "I was numb for a year," Sarah Johnson wrote to me.

For soulmates who spent time with the body of the person who died, the reality was made visible. Because they are often constant companions, many soulmates are present at the moment of (or shortly after) their partner's death. A number of them shared this part of their stories with me, which tells me that not only was the experience unforgettable, it was also something they are still, to some extent, coming to terms with.

You see, when we replay certain moments in our memories and

when we repeat certain stories to ourselves, we do so because we are trying to process them and integrate them into our selves. And even when you reach a place of full cognitive understanding that your soulmate has died, the continued replaying and retelling of the story of the death helps you, over time, understand it more and more deeply, in your heart.

For some soulmates, the experience of watching their partner die was reassuring, if heart-wrenching. Pam wrote, "His eyes were closed, and his breathing was labored. When he took his last breath, he sat up, opened his eyes, and the expression on his face was one of awe and amazement."

For others, the line that marks the transition from life to death comes as a surprising slap in the face, even when the death was anticipated.

Of course, when the death is unexpected, the moment of death can be especially traumatic. "My husband died a sudden death from a ruptured artery," Geralyn Nathe-Evans wrote. "Within minutes we went from the joy of being on the lake on a beautiful June evening to me holding my love as he took his last breath."

In general, soulmate deaths that are sudden, violent, premature, and/or painful and prolonged will give rise to even more complicated grief. In fact, the more traumatic the circumstances of the death, the more

> *"At the funeral home I wanted to take Sharon by the hand and say, 'Come on. Get up. Let's get out of here and go have dinner.'"*
>
> — James Cox

> *"No one knows what it feels like (if you can feel anything). No one talks about death actually happening: Your loved one dying in front of you. And when it's done, finally lying in bed, mouth rigid and open, no longer handsome (poor, dear man), just dead, gone forever. Until that moment, you didn't understand what forever and gone meant: the total desolation."*
>
> — Barbra Wells Fitzgerald

time and energy the surviving soulmate will likely have to dedicate to heroically meeting this mourning need before fully engaging with the remaining five needs that follow. Death is never an easy reality to absorb, but when the circumstances of the death are challenging, thoughts and feelings about the minutes or hours surrounding the death can be all-consuming.

"All in all, we shared ten years. He took his last breath in my arms the day after we celebrated our 7th Valentine's Day as man and wife. It was unexpected and left me in shocked numbness. I couldn't believe that the love of my life had been ripped away from me. One minute he was sleeping soundly at my side, the next he was clutching his chest trying to breathe, and before the paramedics arrived at our house, he was gone."

— Christina Fernández-Morrow

Several grieving soulmates wrote to me about their ongoing struggles truly absorbing the reality of their partners' deaths. Kurt Geiger shared the story of waking up each morning in the early days after his wife's death having forgotten that she had died—then, in the first minute of wakefulness, re-realizing the horrible truth. He felt deep shame over this experience: "How was it possible that someone could forget, even for a second, that their spouse was dead? It was horrifying and shocking that I could have done such a heartless thing. It is bad enough to have lost a spouse, but to have to endure this memory lapse over and over was more than anyone should have to bear."

Yet Kurt's experience is not only common, it is understandable and normal. For soulmates, the reality of their partner's everyday presence and the constant nature of the relationship were so fundamental to their very existence that when the partners are separated by death, the mind has a particularly difficult time adjusting to the new normal. The person who is now missing had typically been a close and tangible presence day in and day out for years, if not decades. How can someone who was *right here* for so long now be just…gone?

Because the reality of the death is so hard to fully acknowledge, you may still find yourself expecting your soulmate to walk through the front door. When you hear the familiar sound of the garage door lifting, you might hold your breath, hoping against hope that the death was a bad dream or illusion somehow. Or you might think you catch glimpses of your soulmate in a crowd or passing car. Grieving soulmates who have these experiences sometimes think they are going crazy. They are not. All of these normal and common experiences are simply signals that they are working on this heroic mourning need.

> *"I miss his kiss on my neck when I am washing dishes and his arms around my shoulders, which made me feel so protected."*
>
> — Ruth Turner

> *"After his passing, I was on autopilot. Just going through the motions. Crying came easy. It wasn't that I was depressed. I was grieving for his voice, his smell, his hugs and kisses."*
>
> — Kathy Madsen

Focusing on the absence is also part of this mourning need. "Where *are* you?" grieving people often ask of their loved ones who have died. The grievers have seen and sometimes spent time with the dead body, attended the visitation and funeral, witnessed the casket being lowered into the ground at the committal or the urn interred in the columbarium, and yet still their minds and hearts cannot grasp the separation.

Mourners also instinctively understand that the body and the soul are not one and the same, so when they ask, "Where *are* you?," they are pleading to know where the soul now resides. They may have acknowledged the physical reality of the death, but they are still struggling with the *meaning* of death (also see Heroic Mourning Need 5: Search for meaning). Has this happened to you?

WHEN YOUR SOULMATE DIES

What all this boils down to is that death is an extremely difficult reality to truly and fully acknowledge when it happens to anyone you love. But when that person is your soulmate, the task is often exponentially more formidable.

IDEAS FOR GRIEVING SOULMATES

For grieving soulmates, heroically encountering this need of mourning means drawing upon at least three of the soulmate characteristics we reviewed in Chapter One.

HONESTY

In our discussion of "Best Friends" in Chapter One, I mentioned the importance of honesty to the soulmate relationship. Likewise, honesty with yourself is essential to meeting this need of mourning.

Linda Albright wrote to me about how she decided to be honest with herself about the death of her husband. "I started saying 'Bob is dead' or 'Bob died' out loud when I was home alone," she said. "There was something about hearing my voice say those words that helped me begin to accept his death. Accepting Bob's death has been the most difficult part of my grief as I write this almost ten months after he died."

Beginning to write and talk to others about your soulmate in the honest past tense can also be a tool to help you work on this need. Mary Potter Kenyon shared with me that journaling helped her begin to meet this need of mourning. "One of the first things I did was to sit down and fill three pages of a journal with everything I was thankful for," she wrote, "most notably the bonus five years I'd shared with David, and the fact that I'd experienced a kind of love that others might spend a lifetime searching for."

Other ideas for honestly confronting the reality of the death include regularly visiting the cemetery or scattering site, sharing news of the death with others who may not yet have heard about it, and working on the other five heroic mourning needs in the chapters to come.

RITUAL

Whenever I meet mourners who are having a hard time acknowledging the reality of a death (usually due to complicating factors, such as sudden or violent death, death of a young person, too many losses in a short period of time, or, as in your case, an unusually close relationship), I encourage them to use three ceremonies spread out over time. Because everyday words and actions are inadequate in the face of death, ceremony—which, like your grief, is also larger than life—can help "dose" you with the reality of the death of your soulmate.

The funeral or memorial service you held for your soulmate was the first ceremony. I hope you were fortunate to have experienced a personalized, meaningful funeral, but if you were not, know that it is never too late to hold another memorial ceremony that better meets your needs.

Ten to twelve months after the funeral—or now, if that milestone has already passed—consider holding a second ceremony. One idea is to get together with close friends and family members at the cemetery, scattering site, or other special place that evokes your soulmate and share memories, prayers, and music.

Then again at approximately a year after the second ceremony, plan a third ceremony. This time you might have a tree planting with close friends and family or an intimate candle-lighting ritual. Place a lit candle in the center of a table and form a circle around the table, with each person holding his or her own small candle. Have each person in turn light his or her candle by holding it to the center candle's flame. As participants light their candles, they are invited to share a memory of the person who died. At the end, play a song or read a poem or prayer in memory of your soulmate.

Such rituals will help meet all of your heroic mourning needs, but they have special power in moving you closer and closer to acknowledging the reality of the death with both your head and your heart.

PERSEVERANCE

For soulmates, fully acknowledging the reality of the death—with the head as well as the heart—will often take much longer than expected. Knowing this early on may help you give yourself permission to work on this need for as long as it takes. Be heroically patient, and when you fail, forgive yourself because your quest is epic, and epic quests involve many failures along the way.

Yet your soulmate relationship may have taught you that perseverance yields rewards. I promise you that this is also true in grief.

Keep in mind that the heroic nature of your mourning quest will likely make it necessary for you to amplify your means of expressing of your grief—for this need and for the other five that follow. Remember, your soulmate grief is oversized, so it will probably take larger and more frequent attempts at expression than griefs you've experienced in the past.

Similarly, your need for rest and self-care in between bouts of mourning will also likely be more intense than is typical. So muster the courage to encounter your grief in a significant way then retreat to care for yourself in a significant way. This grand back-and-forth will slowly, over time, probably become less dramatic for you, but in the meantime, daring to mourn greatly when you have the energy to will help you reap the greatest rewards.

Please write about your progress and struggles so far in acknowledging the reality of your soulmate's death—with both your head and your heart.

CHAPTER FIVE

HEROIC MOURNING NEED 2.

EMBRACE THE PAIN
OF THE LOSS

"I suspect there will come a time in the future when the pain is not so searing and the silence of coming home without Deb not so deafening, but I am still waiting for that time."

— Rosanna Mason, a year after the death

This need of mourning requires all of us who grieve to embrace the pain of loss—something we naturally don't want to do. It can seem easier and more desirable to avoid, repress, or deny the pain of grief than it is to confront it, yet it is in confronting—even befriending— our pain that we learn to reconcile ourselves to it.

Common thoughts and feelings experienced by people encountering this need of mourning include not only aching sadness but also other so-called "dark" emotions, such as anger, rage, guilt, and regret. So when I use the catchall term "pain," I mean whatever combination of these and other thoughts and feelings might be hurting you inside.

In the Introduction we briefly discussed the uniquely blazing nature of the pain of soulmate grief. Many of the surviving soulmates who wrote to me said that the agony they felt after the death of their partners was exponentially worse than the pain they had felt after the deaths of other significant people in their lives. While all of us must meet this challenging need after the death of someone loved, grieving soulmates often feel crushed by it. The pain is so intense, so severe, so constant, and so relentless, often they feel as if they can barely survive.

And yet…over time, intermittently, slowly, and with the support of others, embrace your soulmate-sized pain you must.

In fact, when any thought or emotion arises in grief, we need to learn to experience it. To eventually heal it, we must get into the

> *"I had no idea what was happening to me when he died. I couldn't think logically. I would freak out at very small things that would go wrong. I often cried uncontrollably to an almost panic state. I experienced physical pain in my heart. It felt like someone had taken over my body, and I stood back and watched in horror what was happening."*
>
> — Karen Steen

practice of acknowledging it and feeling it.

We're good at doing this when it comes to love. We welcome our feelings of connection and joy, right? We revel in them. We bask in them. So when the natural sequels to these feelings follow, we must experience them as well—*because that is the only way through them.*

As the priest Robert Benson has said, "To embrace one's brokenness, whatever it looks like, whatever has caused it, carries within it the possibility that one might come to embrace one's healing."

Besides, I would ask, what choice do you as a grieving soulmate really have? Try as you might to distract or deny, you can't help but frequently *feel* the pain, sadness, despair, and regret anyway. Working to ignore or suppress these hurtful feelings doesn't make them go away. Not really. Instead, what eventually happens is that any unacknowledged, unembraced, and unexpressed thoughts and feelings you carry inside you begin to insidiously mute, undermine, and even destroy the remainder of your life. The psychic black hole caused by what I call "carried grief" typically manifests over time as ongoing problems such as depression, anxiety, substance abuse, and/ or relationship troubles.

Unfortunately, our culture colludes with the temptation to carry grief. Misunderstanding the true nature and role of suffering, it tends to encourage the denial of or distraction from pain. It's also really uncomfortable with the expression of pain, i.e. mourning. If you openly express your feelings of grief, misinformed friends might well tell you to "be strong" or "keep it together." If, on the other hand, you do remain "strong" and "in control," you may be congratulated for "doing well" with your grief.

The trouble is, we have it all backward. Doing well with grief actually means becoming well acquainted with pain.

Of course, you can't embrace your pain all at once—it's too big, too overwhelming, too deadly. Instead, you will need to "dose" yourself with the hurt, doing what I call "sitting in the wound of your grief" in short stints. At other times you will need to distract yourself from the pain of the loss. I call this normal and necessary back-and-forth "evade-encounter"—you step away from your pain for a short time to catch your breath and regroup, then, when it arises again, you step toward it and embrace it. You evade, then you encounter. You encounter, then you evade. It's the only way to both embrace and survive the agony of soulmate grief.

> *"A widow's grief is an emotional firestorm, with hundreds of fires, both large and small, her children's as well as her own. The massive blazes—birthdays, family celebrations, an 'angelversary'—are predictable events, ones a widow can prepare for. She can grab flame-retardant gear and get through some fires with minor injuries. But then there are the brush fires that spring up unexpectedly. The smell of roses, any Beatles song, or a Facebook post that displays the joys of an intact family can sear a widow's heart and rip through her soul. It's okay to nurse these wounds, to share the pain and accept comfort from supporters."*
>
> — Allison Wysota

What's more, you must also keep in mind that pain in grief is not only emotional pain. When you grieve, you often experience pain physically, cognitively, socially, and spiritually, as well. Grieving bodies hurt; grieving brains have a hard time concentrating and thinking. Social relationships become strained, and beliefs are tested.

Our cultural biases toward pain and suffering will likely make it hard for you to heroically mourn your pain. We are taught from an early age that such feelings are bad and that happiness and joy are good. The truth is, however, that all of these feelings simply *are.* One is just as much a part of the human experience as the other. And, counterintuitively, learning to befriend and express pain and suffering is the very process that can lead you back to happiness and joy.

> *"Suffering is part of the fabric of a human incarnation, as is death. And not feeling that death is the enemy, but that death is part of a process—just like autumn and winter aren't enemies of spring and summer. Now part of that is aided a lot by understanding and deepening faith in the fact that there is soul or spiritual context in which physical existence dwells. And as you develop that spiritual context and appreciate that suffering from within that context is the stuff of growth, then under those conditions you are much more capable of handling the physical conditions even though your heart is breaking."*
>
> — Ram Dass

IDEAS FOR GRIEVING SOULMATES

For grieving soulmates, heroically encountering this need of mourning means calling on several of the soulmate characteristics we reviewed in Chapter One.

VULNERABILITY

Just as you opened yourself to your soulmate's love, you must now open yourself to your pain over your soulmate's death. Your pain is massive, so making yourself vulnerable to it will take equally massive courage.

Learning to sit with your pain is central to this mourning need. When you feel the hurt coming on, try mindfulness techniques to be "with" the pain. If possible, stop what you are doing, close your eyes, breathe deeply, and allow the pain to wash over you. I call it "sitting in the wound of your grief."

Grieving soulmate Jan Wilson suggests setting a timer to dose yourself with the pain. "When you sink into a hole, set a timer for 5 to 15 minutes and allow yourself to feel whatever feelings you are experiencing," she wrote. "When the timer rings, get up, get moving, get going."

Denise Meehan advocates for taking a break from the yin of your pain as often as every 10 minutes to affirm the yang of your love. "When the difficult days or moments come, know that you were blessed to have loved someone so deeply," she wrote. "So if it is every ten minutes, just smile and say to yourself, 'Today, it will be every ten minutes.'"

Crying is also part of allowing yourself to be vulnerable, especially in a culture that too often sees tears as a sign of weakness. If you feel tears coming on, by all means, cry. Cry as long and as hard and as often as you need to. Not only will your heart and soul thank you, but your body will too. That's because human tears carry stress chemicals out of the body. If you allow yourself to be vulnerable to crying, you will feel the counterbalancing experience of relief and release afterward.

"Crying is like vomiting," said Karen Goebel. "The urge is there. It hurts to hold it back. When the tears come, it's such a relief to finally release them. You feel better after a good cry. You wonder why you held it in so long."

> *"A person providing grief support asked my primary emotion—it wasn't anger, hate, guilt, denial. It was fear—the fear of how I would get through each day without my partner, my soulmate."*
>
> — Don Mueller

> *"When one's soul is shattered, healing does not come quickly or easily."*
>
> — Debra Milligan

> *"Cry, then laugh.*
> *Despair, then hang on.*
> *Be scared, then look for hope.*
> *Reflect, then look forward.*
> *Be angry, then forgive.*
> *And don't forget to forgive yourself."*
>
> — Don Mueller

Laura Renker agreed. "When Les died without warning, it felt like an amputation, like a large part of me had been removed," she wrote. "I have had to learn to make friends with grief and sorrow, and to feel at least some sense of comfort with shedding copious amounts of tears on a daily basis."

Of course, crying is only one means of expressing pain. Other emotional releases include yelling, pacing, throwing things, writing, and talking. (The only rule being: never hurt yourself or others or destroy valuable property.)

"I always thought that crying, being mad or upset was a sign of weakness," wrote Janet Tompkins. "It made me feel so much better to know that if I needed to scream, I should scream."

Don Mueller opened up within the safe confines of a journal. "I started writing in a journal," he wrote. "I am a private person, and I needed an outlet to express my difficult feelings without burdening my children or extended family and friends. I didn't shut them out, but I also needed a private outlet. On tough days, I would develop a chart with two columns: challenges and new beginnings. In working on this chart, I would see progress in my grief, small or large."

KINDNESS

You learned and practiced the art of kindness throughout your soulmate relationship. In fact, perhaps your soulmate relationship gave you the longest opportunity to refine your capacity for kindness over time.

Now it is time to lavish your kindness on yourself. As you do the naturally arduous and draining work of embracing your larger-than-life pain, you must, as we've said, balance those efforts with exceptional self-care.

In what ways can you practice self-kindness as you are mourning? One way to start coming up with a self-care menu is to take inventory of all the ways in which your soulmate was kind to you. After you've compiled the list, consider which of the items brought you the most happiness, then consider how to receive similar care in other ways and from other people. No, it will not be the same as when your soulmate offered the kindness, but it may still be helpful to you. For example, let's say that your soulmate gave you flowers now and then, and those flowers brought you joy. Perhaps now you yourself can pick up a bunch of flowers occasionally to place throughout your home.

Another way to practice self-kindness is to treat yourself every single day to at least one thing you would normally consider an indulgence. What are such things for you? Ideas might include a nap, a game of golf, a manicure or pedicure, reading a novel, binge-watching a TV show, a take-out meal from your favorite restaurant, lunch with a friend, attending a concert, or getting a massage. Never forget that mourning heroes such as yourself need and deserve many rewards.

> *"I found exercise to be incredibly helpful. I had lost a significant amount of weight because I just couldn't eat, but the gym helped me regain and my body felt better and re-energized, which helped improve my mood."*
>
> — Victoria Muñoz-Schmitt

Of course, self-kindness must also include fulfilling your obligations for items 5 through 9 in the Grieving Soulmate's Code of Honor (pg. 63). If you aren't caring for yourself well physically, cognitively, emotionally, socially, and spiritually, you are not bestowing the kindness on yourself that you deserve, and you will not be able to mourn well and move forward on your quest for healing.

COMPANIONSHIP

The expression of pain often requires a good listener. People who will listen without judging or feeling the need to take away your pain are good friends in grief. You talk; they listen and empathize.

I've noticed that about one-third of the people in our lives are capable of showing up with a loving heart and a ministry of presence. Another third can't really help in this way but don't hurt us either. And the final third are often toxic and harmful to our healing. They may tell us to quit mourning or declare that we're doing it wrong.

This "rule of thirds" is good to keep in mind. We should steer clear of that last third, and when we're fortunate to meet someone in the first third, someone who's blessed with a ministry of presence, we'll know whom to turn to when we need companionship on our journey.

Of course, I understand that you have lost your closest companion. This is a significant part of the pain of your grief—one I am here to validate and bear witness to. What I want you to consider now is that cultivating new companions and/or strengthening bonds with existing friends will not only help you meet this heroic need of mourning, it will enhance all aspects of your life from here forward. Your soulmate relationship taught you companionship skills. Now it is your challenge to use those skills to build relationships with others.

Pets, too, can provide companionship. They gladly offer their constant presence and unconditional love. Grieving soulmate Jean Brody wrote to me about her companion animals who helped her during her times of pain:

"The key to my ultimate survival besides finding a life purpose was my two cats. Possibly only animal lovers would understand this, but without my two beloved cats to hold, sleep with, and talk to, I would have suffered a lot more. I could absolutely depend on them to push close to my body when the loneliness of dark days and empty nights threatened to disconnect me from who I had always been. Pets offer no "pat answers," no promises that things will get better, no instructions to "be strong." They do not have distractions that humans have, and when they sense that you are sad, you truly become their focus. All you need to do for them is feed them and let them help you. Try it."

RITUALS

Just as daily rituals elevated the sense of love and meaning in your routines with your soulmate, so too can rituals help you now with heroically mourning your pain.

Rituals give your body and heart something to *do* when you are

> *"I try to keep to the same routine as when he was physically here. At times I feel his presence and I will wear one of his T-shirts to feel his arms around me. I speak to him every day to tell him about my day and what's going on. I also ask God to give me the strength to make it through tomorrow."*
>
> — Carol Bronson

grieving. The funeral is an essential ritual of grief immediately following a death, but even long after the funeral, small daily rituals can provide meaningful action and structure. When normal, random daily activity and everyday words don't seem like enough to express the magnitude of your pain, turn to ritual.

When you are hurting, you can choose to embrace your pain while surrounded by the strong support of ritual. You can light a candle and sit in quiet meditation or prayer. You can finger prayer beads. You can attend a spiritual service. You can practice yoga. You can walk a labyrinth or a favorite nature trail. You may listen to a certain song on your earbuds while you complete one of these activities. You might want to start your ritual with a certain phrase or centering thought, either spoken aloud or silently in your mind, and end with the same thought or a prayer.

Grieving soulmate Patti Stahl told me that during the long, cold winter after her sister-in-law died, followed closely by the unexpected death of her sister-in-law's husband, who was Patti's soulmate brother, Patti reveled during that long, cold winter in the nightly ritual of turning inward. "I cherished my working 'hibernation,'" she wrote. "I worked every day but went home, put

my lounging pajamas on, and hibernated. I appreciated the solitude.
I appreciated being lazy, warm, and safe. I appreciated my Dove dark
chocolate with almonds. I appreciated my husband's understanding.
I appreciated my kind boss, who gently tolerated my emotions. I
truly appreciated being left alone as much as possible. I appreciated
the peace and quiet."

Please write about your progress and struggles so far in embracing the pain
of your loss. In what ways do you regularly express your pain outside of
yourself?

CHAPTER SIX

HEROIC MOURNING NEED 3.
REMEMBER YOUR
SOULMATE

"Keep telling the love story to anyone who will listen. It brings back the beauty, light, and love. Until we meet again, sweet Edwin."

— Joyce Neikirk

After your soulmate dies, no one has to tell you to remember him or her. Your every waking moment may be filled with memories—and your dreams, too.

Do you find yourself constantly replaying memories—of the last time you spoke, of the day of the death, of the first time you met, of special moments that the two of you shared? Do memories arise every time you move through a room or put on a jacket or drive past a certain place?

Such replay is normal and natural. It is part of your need to fully acknowledge the reality of the death. It is also central to all the other mourning needs we are reviewing in this chapter.

Your memories are your treasures and your consolation. While I understand they are absolutely no substitute for the living, breathing presence of your soulmate, they are what you have left. They are the legacy of your love and your time spent together.

And while it is likely that not every memory you have of your soulmate is happy or pleasant, all memories are precious, for they are the best that we as human beings can do to, as the song says, save time in a bottle.

While you are probably already remembering your soulmate often, what you may not understand is that this remembering is good and necessary. Whenever you remember, you are telling yourself the story of your relationship. Bit by bit, you are assembling a cohesive narrative that begins at the beginning, muddles through the middle, and ends at the end.

We tell ourselves stories to make sense of our lives; you are telling yourself the story of your soulmate relationship to make sense—physically, cognitively, emotionally, socially, and spiritually—of what happened.

As we discussed in Chapter One, many of you were fortunate enough to enjoy numerous years and even decades together with your soulmate. That's a lot of memories! One grieving soulmate who wrote to me, Pat Lillicrop, said that she and her husband, Cliff, knew each other from the moment of their births because their parents were close friends. "I have no place in my life, my mind, or my physical presence to go back to where Cliff wasn't," Pat wrote. "He has always just been—just like me."

As Pat knows so well, the longevity of many soulmate relationships can complicate this need of mourning because most of your memories may be, in one way or another, tied up with your life together with the precious person who died.

SOULMATES WITH DEMENTIA

The loss of a soulmate to dementia and Alzheimer's featured prominently in a number of the grieving soulmate letters I received. These diseases slowly but inexorably steal our loved ones away from us while they are still alive.

If you are among those who suffered the death of a soulmate who was affected by dementia—or perhaps whose soulmate is still alive but has already been significantly diminished by the disease—your grief journey will be complicated in unique ways. I urge you to connect with others who have lost a soulmate to dementia as you are heroically mourning your loss.

I would also like to mention that Dr. Edward Shaw wrote to me in the form of a beautiful essay about his wife, Rebecca, who became debilitated by early Alzheimer's in her 50s. She still lives, but her decline over the past decade has been heartbreaking. Recently she crossed a line that is terrible for her soulmate: she no longer remembers Edward.

And so, Edward, who remains her caregiver, told me in his essay that he has "developed a new focus: to court Rebecca and win her heart as I had nearly four decades ago." He has begun dating her again. I will let his poignant closing words stand in beautiful testament to the power of soulmate love:

"During a recent evening," he wrote, "as I tucked her into bed and turned the light out, planning to get some work done in the next room, Rebecca whispered to me, 'Do you think you'll be coming to bed soon?' I turned around and saw an expectant look in her eyes. 'Can I sleep next to you tonight?' I asked, slipping under the covers, feeling tears of joy. I returned her gaze and saw the woman I've been in love with for so many years. I kissed her forehead, thanking God for a moment that I knew wouldn't last. And maybe, just maybe, Rebecca was falling in love with me all over again."

Remembering your soulmate is often a bittersweet experience, of course. Every time you remember something about the person who died, you are simultaneously forced to confront the reality of the death. The very act of remembering is a counterpoint to the lack of the person's presence in the now. You remember how it *was* because it no longer *is*. In this way, even joyful memories can become extremely painful.

That's why some people might advise you *not* to remember your soulmate. They know that remembering can cause pain, and they are trying to protect you. And so, contaminated by our mourning-avoiding culture, they may encourage you to put away photos and quickly dispatch with your soulmate's personal belongings. They may urge you to "put the past in the past" and "move on." Such people are usually well-intentioned but also sadly misinformed.

Even when it is painful, remembering is essential to your present grief as well as your future happiness. I often say that remembering the past makes hoping for the future possible, and actively engaging with and sharing your memories makes healing possible.

IDEAS FOR GRIEVING SOULMATES

Dear Larry,

I miss you so much. You were my companion, my friend, and my love. You were gone so quickly, and I am so sorry I didn't get to say goodbye. I am now looking forward to heaven more than ever. I will see you again, and we will have no more pain or sorrow, thanks to Jesus.

I am doing things daily that would make you proud. Thank you for making me more confident in myself. You brought out the best in me and encouraged me to follow my dreams and talents.

I will never forget you. You will always be a part of me. Thank you so much for taking good care of me and loving me. My time on this earth will be short, so I will enjoy life as you would want me to; but I look forward to seeing you again.

Love,

Tammy (Cranston)

To help grievers meet this mourning need, I routinely recommend activities such as creating a memory book, filling a memory box, and writing down as well as verbally sharing stories of the person who died. This is good counsel for you as well. As Debra Milligan shared with me, it helped her to "talk about Lee to anyone who would listen, make a photo album of treasured times, and honor him with a scholarship at our local university." Essentially, the more routine remembering you do, the better.

Listening to music can also be a good way to conjure memories and embrace feelings. Susan Robison mentioned this in her letter to me:

"While listening to the songs that were played at his funeral, I do a lot of thinking and remembering the good times we had together. It is a comfort to me. We were married 33 years, and he was my life. I enjoy thinking about the good times we had over the years. I like listening to the music we used to listen to, and I love holding his pillow at night."

Speaking of pillows, here I must also mention "linking objects" and their importance to memory work in grief. Linking objects are special items that belonged to the person who died or represent your relationship in some way. A favorite jacket, a wedding band or other jewelry, a robe or slippers, a special gardening tool, a beloved book or piece of art—these and any number of other things might be a linking object. I call them linking objects because they serve as a physical link to a person who is no longer present.

> *"Oftentimes, friends would suggest I put all the photos that reminded me of my husband away because it would help me feel better. But I love all the memories."*
>
> — Karen Steen

Linking objects can soothe you but also help you remember. They are often good company in grief, and I encourage you to use them liberally in your quest for healing. Because of contamination from our mourning-avoiding culture, some people might tell you that you need to get rid of such objects as quickly as possible. They are wrong. Only if and when you are ready do you need to discard anything that belonged to your soulmate who died, and you will always want to keep some special linking objects.

A LINKING OBJECT SOULMATE STORY

"I was unable to part with any of my husband's possessions other than to give certain treasured items to loved ones. However one day I passed a closet that contained all of the suits he had worn for work before he retired 10 years earlier. I called Project COPE, whose mission is to 'make second chances count' by providing re-entry support to select ex-offenders, including helping them find work. I gathered all of David's work clothes, and I typed a note to place in each coat pocket. It read:

The man who owned this suit before you was named David. He was a man with a large capacity to love and who was loved by everyone he worked with. He was a good listener, and when he talked to you, he made you feel that what you had to say was important. He was a happy and contented man who woke up every day and tried to make the world a better place.

David died very suddenly in June and left behind a wonderful legacy. He will be greatly missed. It would make him very happy to think that his clothes might help someone to feel good about himself as he tries to gain meaningful work and begin a new start in life. So please think of David when you wear this. We hope it brings you peace and good luck as you go forward.

Two months later Project COPF honored David in a newsletter article that said, 'Miraculously, David's clothes fit many of our partners, who were eager to wear them. In their new threads, each stood a little taller and felt much more confident. And who knows? Perhaps David's legacy and strong work ethic wore off on our partners because all but one is now employed!'

I hope this story will be an inspiration to honor your loved ones by helping others. It was a true blessing for me."

— Joy Sterneck

But because your soulmate grief is especially challenging, and because your memories may play such an extensive role in your grief experience, for you I would also suggest going "above and beyond" in remembering your soulmate who died if you feel so inclined. While the following ideas are certainly not necessary, you might find one or more of them helpful to you:

- Start a memory diary. Whenever a new memory of your soulmate arises or is shared with you by another person, write it down.

- Have a blanket or stuffed animal made from your soulmate's favorite clothing.

- Take out an ad in the newspaper on your soulmate's birthday or the anniversary of the death.

- Have bracelets, t-shirts, or tote bags made that memorialize your soulmate in some way and give one to everyone who misses him or her.

- Write and publish a book about your soulmate relationship. Or make a movie.
- Get a tattoo of your soulmate's name or likeness.
- Decorate your Christmas tree with soulmate memorabilia and photos.

Do you see what I mean? You might decide that big and bold memory activities are the only ones that can begin to do your soulmate relationship justice.

In addition, heroically encountering this need of mourning also means calling on at least two of the soulmate characteristics we reviewed in Chapter One.

COMPANIONSHIP

This heroic need of mourning is not just about remembering—it is also about converting your relationship with the person who died from one of presence to one of memory. Because your relationship with your soulmate was likely so much about companionship and presence, this may be an especially challenging part of this mourning need for you to work on.

Consider, though, that you now have the opportunity to make your memories of your soulmate your constant companions. You might do this by wearing a locket containing your soulmate's photo, carrying pictures in your purse or wallet, displaying many photos in your home, watching home movies, or carrying a special keepsake in your pocket at all times. While of course such methods are no substitute for the companionship of your soulmate who died, they will help you begin the hard work of building a relationship of memory versus presence.

Of course, grieving soulmates who believe in life after death understand that their soulmates still exist somewhere. That means they can and often do maintain a relationship of sorts. Instead of converting the relationship from presence to memory, they work on converting the relationship from presence to temporary absence.

These soulmates use activities such as talking out loud to the person who died, writing them letters, and blowing kisses heavenward as a means of acknowledging the reality of the death and embracing the pain of the loss while blending those needs with changing the form of the relationship.

SHARED VALUES

What does remembering have to do with shared values? A lot, it turns out.

Grieving soulmates often find meaning in reviewing the beliefs and values they shared with their soulmate and then finding ways to remember the person who died that align with those beliefs and values. The surviving soulmate may continue to volunteer for organizations that the two of them supported, for example, or recommit to certain activities or experiences that both of them loved.

John Sammons said, "Besides volunteering, other avenues I have used to honor my soulmate is by donating in her memory to cancer research and other worthy causes, placing special artwork in her memory, and planting a tree in her memory on the first anniversary of her death. In the future, I plan to continue donating my time and resources in my soulmate's memory and to the glory of God our Father."

Other grieving soulmates inventory the values and causes that the person who died held especially dear and work to honor them in the soulmate's memory.

For example, Sharon Triano-Kott wrote to me about how she honored her best friend after she died:

"I realized I needed to honor my friend in ways that she demonstrated were important to her. She readily gave to others with no expectations of return. I donated her clothes to someone who could benefit from them. I cooked dinner for her son and made sure he was ok. I am attempting to set up a scholarship for a senior citizen who loves swimming as my friend did and is in financial need. As I completed these things, I felt the pieces coming together. These acts helped me honor her life and legacy. They also helped me to live life to the fullest today."

Please write about your progress and struggles so far in remembering your soulmate who died and converting your relationship from one of presence to one of memory.

CHAPTER SEVEN

HEROIC MOURNING NEED 4.

DEVELOP A NEW SELF-IDENTITY

"The daily grind comes with daily and moment-to-moment reminders of his absence. He will not pick up the kids. He will not wash the dishes after you cook. He will not mow the lawn, shovel the snow, fix the leaky roof, soothe a heartbroken teenage daughter. He will not walk the dogs or plan this winter's ski vacation."

— Karen Goebel

Soulmates are by definition among the most closely bonded people in the world. The stronger the attachment and the more constant the day-to-day companionship that was part of the relationship, the more soulmates' self-identities tend to be bound up with one another's. Like the double helix of DNA, they spiral around one another with elegant beauty and great strength. Their individual strands are linked in countless places.

It's no wonder that many soulmates think less of themselves as individuals and more of themselves as part of a couple. At least to some extent, they are half of a whole entity that interacts with others and with the world in certain ways. They, as a duo, participate in *these* activities. They shop at *these* stores. They eat dinner at *this* time. They move through their lives on that bicycle-built-for-two that we talked about before.

When soulmates aren't together, they are often playing complementary roles, separately. The two partners typically divvy up tasks and responsibilities. One washes the dishes while the other dries. Or one does the dishes while the other mows the lawn. One pays the bills; the other does the shopping. One handles the social calendar; the other stays in touch with family. One is good at planning; the other is good at leading. Usually they seem to find a satisfying and often joyful balance on the seesaw of life, and when one of them dies, the seesaw tips, sending the surviving soulmate crashing.

But regardless of how much time you and your soulmate spent together and how many daily activities you shared, your soulmate who died was a part of you, and you were a part of him or her. You may feel that when your soulmate died, a substantial part of you died too.

The intertwining nature of soulmate self-identities makes this heroic mourning need particularly challenging for grieving soulmates. "When she died, I wanted to die myself," wrote Charles Stackhouse. "I was no longer a husband. I was no longer a worker, since I had quit my job to care for her. I had lost all purpose and identity."

Questions grieving soulmates often ask as they are working on this need include: Who will I talk to? How will I cook and eat alone? How will I fill my days? What about our house? Will I still travel? What about finances? Who will take care of me when I am sick or need medical care?

It strikes me that there are two overlapping phases to this mourning need. For grieving soulmates, there is the slow process of relinquishing many aspects of their old self-identities—the parts that were connected to the person who died—and then there is the slow process of rebuilding their new self-identities. Both phases are painful and challenging. Both require heroic effort.

What's more, our self-identities are both inner and outer. Inside our minds and hearts, we see and think of ourselves in certain ways. Outside of ourselves, other people see and think of us in different ways, and our awareness of their expectations is also part of our self-identities. After the death of your soulmate, then, both your inner and outer self-identities are forced to begin to adapt.

For grieving soulmates, the social role changes often come as a shock. You may have gone from being a "wife" or "husband" to a "widow" or "widower." Even if you were not married, you are now faced with the idea of being single again. The ways in which your friends, family, neighbors, and community have thought of and related to you, and the way you have thought of yourself, are in the painful process of re-forming. What do these category and conceptual changes mean to you and your life—from both the outside in and the inside out?

> *"Widowhood is a loss with many layers. It is a loss of love, partnership, and friendship, compounded by the loss of identity of being someone's spouse. It is a role I didn't relinquish four years ago; it was taken from me. I was robbed, and there will be no justice."*
>
> — Allison Wysota

And what about the ways in which you interacted with the world outside of your relationship with your soulmate? How are those changing as a result of your loss? Now that you are no longer half of a whole in your day-to-day life, you are probably doing some things differently. You may be shouldering tasks and roles that used to be taken care of by the person who died. Perhaps you are slowly learning to step outside of ingrained ways of doing things and dipping your toe into new possibilities. Or you may be taking comfort in old habits while finding ways to adapt them for one person instead of two.

CONTINUED INTERTWINING

Many grieving soulmates do not believe it is necessary to completely disentangle themselves from their partners who died. Quite a few of the grieving soulmates who shared their stories with me emphasized, in one way or another, that their soulmates continue to be an important part of their self-identities.

"Just as he helped shape my life as a teenager of 19, he is continuing to do so in this the latter part of my life," wrote Ruth Turner. "Because of him, even though I still wish he were here to share these years, I am leading a fulfilling life helping other widows and widowers to do the same and showing them that they *can* go on to a 'new normal' although it is a different normal…so I thank him for my memories and his guidance."

Geralyn Nathe-Evans echoes Ruth. "While our society has given me the title of 'widow,' I have not yet come to wrap my head or heart around that term," she wrote. "I am still Dave's wife. I continue to live with my heart so connected to his being, and I continue to know his presence in my life from beyond."

Author Mitch Albom famously wrote, "Death ends a life, not a relationship." I wholeheartedly agree. Geralyn and Ruth are proof of this truth. In Chapter Six, when we explored the need to remember the person who died, we talked about the need to convert the relationship from one of presence to one of memory. We also noted that for grieving soulmates who believe in an afterlife, the challenge is, instead, converting the relationship from one of presence to one of temporary absence. If you are among this latter group, I would simply encourage you to be aware of the need to nurture self-efficacy, which is your belief in your own ability to take action and thrive.

Though your instincts and beliefs might reassure you that your self-identity continues to be entwined with that of your soulmate, I hope you will not use this as an excuse to grieve but not mourn and heal. The danger is not in continuing your relationship with the person who died: the danger is in hiding from life's ongoing possibilities because of it. A foundational philosophy of this book is that your life is not effectively over after your soulmate dies. Instead, I strongly believe that through heroic mourning, you can find meaning and joy in your new life again without the physical presence of your soulmate.

So if you have a continuing relationship of some kind with your soulmate—a relationship that gives you comfort, meaning, and joy—I am glad. Please, please do not fool yourself into believing that this relationship can or should be your everything until you die, however. Choosing to shut yourself off from new experiences and other close relationships is to live a shadow life. It is to squander the privilege of living. Instead, I urge you to grieve fully, mourn fully, and go on to live fully. Your changed, full life will certainly include a relationship of one kind or another with your soulmate who died—but that relationship should eventually play softly but steadily in the background while your present life unfolds with meaning and purpose in the foreground.

Self-transformation is never easy, but it's especially wrenching when it is something you desperately wish with every breath weren't happening. It is not uncommon for grievers to feel angry, helpless, frustrated, inadequate, and/or afraid as they work on this mourning need. Uncomfortable feelings of heightened dependence on others are also typical, as are struggles with self-worth.

You may find yourself lashing out at others, too, as you begin to fathom the extent of the damage done by the death. This is understandable. The very core of who you are has been torn apart. Dottie Blun Chambers wrote to me that after the death of her father, his soulmate—Dottie's mother—"lost herself." During this time, the mother said and did many hurtful things. If you have found yourself saying and doing hurtful things as you confronted the annihilation of your former self-identity, try to forgive yourself and ask forgiveness of others. You are doing the best you can.

Also, it's OK if there are things you *don't* miss about your soulmate. Don Mueller mentioned he doesn't miss the backseat driver, having to fix all the technology in the house, shopping for clothing, TV shows he didn't like, etc. There can be an understandable sense of newfound freedom—especially if your soulmate suffered an extended illness—even though it is a freedom you would never choose.

I would also like to note that because of the strength of the soulmate bond, grieving soulmates, like grieving parents, sometimes even continue to worry about the self-identities of their loved ones who have died. In other words, they continue to wonder or be concerned about their soulmates' well-being wherever they are right now and/or what their soulmates are missing out on here on earth. Have you been feeling any ongoing worry, concern, or regret for your soulmate?

Donna Thompson has. She wrote to me that even though she has found meaning again in music, dancing, nature, and spending time with her children and grandchildren since the death of her husband, she still feels bad for *him*. "These were and are some of my favorite

> *"Four years later, I've learned that I am stronger than I ever thought possible or gave myself credit for. Widows need to own their grief. The grief establishes permanent residency. It might change form, get easier at different stages, but it will always be there—lying just beneath the surface of the skin, waiting to be awakened."*
>
> — Allison Wysota

things," she said, "but my most very favorite was my husband. It is all a shame that he is not sitting next to me in front of the fire. I don't feel sorry for myself—just him."

While it may be too soon for you to consider this possibility, I will also add that many grieving people ultimately discover that as they work on this need to develop a new self-identity, they discover some positive aspects of their changed selves. They may be surprised to meet a new confidence in themselves, for example. They may uncover a more caring, kind, and sensitive part of themselves. They may develop an assertive part of their identities that empowers them to go on living fully even though they continue to feel a deep sense of loss.

People can and do change for the better. People grow, and devastating grief can be the catalyst. It is growth that requires a deep sacrifice, however—a sacrifice no one would choose if undoing it were possible. I know that, and you know that. But because undoing death is NOT possible, growth through grief is the best possible outcome.

IDEAS FOR GRIEVING SOULMATES

Yes, as Karen makes clear, heroically mourning this need does not happen quickly or easily. It definitely requires perseverance—one of the key soulmate skills we covered in Chapter One.

Here are two other soulmate characteristics you might consider turning to as you work on this challenging need:

ADVENTURE

In the Quest Commitment you signed on page 56, you declared your intent to heroically mourn so that you can find meaning in your

> *"I struggled for more than a year every single day trying to figure out who I was now, what I should be doing, if anything would make me smile and be happy again."*
>
> — Karen Steen

continued living. You agreed not to settle for the shadow-life of carried grief. You promised not to die while you are alive.

The adventurer's skills you practiced as a soulmate will serve you well in your quest to honor your commitment. In your relationship with your soulmate, you looked to the future with fortitude and hope. I challenge you to work toward doing the same now.

Grieving soulmate Julie Lynn McIntyre told me that as he was dying, her beloved husband urged her to continue truly living without him. His hope and belief in the grand possibilities for her future life without him became the catalyst she needed:

Before he died, Michael challenged me to use this future time to take on all the projects and challenges that I had set aside as a result of creating the life that we both wanted to have. He encouraged me to go on and gave his blessing, which has remained with me as the greatest peace in his passing. In my deep grief, I began to take art classes, and I noted that I could once again see in color rather than the shades of gray that had become a way of life without my soulmate.

A wise friend suggested that I consider combining my love of counseling and art and become an art therapist. It seemed like a daunting challenge in my mid-fifties. Eight years and two degrees later, I graduated as an art therapist. I continue to work to this day delivering programming to those who are palliative and bereaved as well as teaching how to integrate the arts into hospice and bereavement programs in a community college. I truly love my work and feel that I was born to do this. I am sad that Michael didn't get to live longer, that we didn't grow into our golden years together, but I will never regret the woman I have become and the lives that I have touched as a result of this unfolding journey.

It is the relationship that we shared for thirty years as soulmates that gave me the confidence and comfort with death and dying to make a difference. I am forever grateful for the joyful love of life that I shared with Michael and his parting gift of confidence that I go forward in faith without him.

Do you see how Julie's sense of life as an ongoing adventure, bolstered by Michael's support, created a path for her to slowly recreate her self-identity and find meaning again? Julie's story is a particularly remarkable example. It's not necessary for you to go back to school and start a new career to develop a new self-identity. What is necessary is to search inside yourself for who you are without your soulmate.

SENSE OF HUMOR

That appreciation for laughter you may have shared with your soulmate? You can also use it now as you encounter the many absurdities of life alone.

The first time you attempt to do something that used to be your soulmate's responsibility, if it doesn't go well, consider the humor in it. Imagine your soulmate watching you, laughing, and shaking his or her head. If you feel like crying instead, then by all means, cry. Just remember that crying and laughing at the same time is often a healing combination.

Seeking out laughter in your day-to-day activities is another approach to try. What almost never fails to make you laugh? Whatever or whoever it is, consider adding a dose of it to your daily routine.

A SENSE OF PRIVILEGE AND HONOR

Today you are still alive. None of us knows exactly how many days we have left on this earth, but we do have today. Your self is here, now. If you try, you can attach your changing self-identity to an appreciation for this fact.

In other words, if you felt a sense of privilege and honor to have experienced a soulmate relationship, I believe you likewise have an obligation—to yourself and to your soulmate—to live out the rest of your days with a sense of privilege and honor.

> "My life and yours changes dramatically, I'm no longer a wife. I'm no longer part of a couple. The list goes on and on. What I still am is a Mom, a Nana, a woman who is leading a grief ministry at church. I am trying to help others on their grief journeys and have met some wonderful people who have now become my friends. I am also a woman who daily thanks God and tries to be more grateful than sad."
>
> — Shayne Kemp

This does not mean you do not grieve deeply and mourn heroically! This does not mean you deny the excruciating pain! What it means is that even as you grieve and mourn, you also work to hold on to that sense of privilege and honor you developed during your soulmate relationship. You hurt AND you appreciate each day as much as you can. You struggle AND you have gratitude. You find ways to do both.

No matter your struggles with self-identity, I want you to know I believe in you. I believe in your capacity to change, heal, and grow. You are capable of amazing things. After all, you're a soulmate.

Please write about your experiences with self-identity since the death of your soulmate. In what ways are you actively and outwardly expressing your thoughts and feelings about changes in self-identity?

CHAPTER EIGHT

HEROIC MOURNING NEED 5.

SEARCH FOR MEANING

"I've tried to tell myself how blessed I was to have him in my life. But 16 months later, I still scream. I still shout, 'Why?'"

— Janet Tompkins

Your soulmate relationship was a significant part of what gave your life meaning. In fact, thanks to your soulmate relationship, you were privileged to experience more meaning in life than many people ever do. And yet despite this fact, it is normal and natural for you to now be reassessing what all of it meant.

Why do we live? Why do we die? Why were you paired in a soulmate relationship when others are not? Why did your partner have to die first? Why is there even such a thing as a soulmate relationship if it always has to end with such devastation? How are you supposed to find meaning in life again after your soulmate dies?

"Knowing my children will live their young adult lives without their mother is hard. My wife's young death means our grandchildren will not know their grandmother."

— Don Mueller

These and other Big Questions are no doubt on your pondering list these days—and maybe your raging, despairing, and feeling-like-you're-going-crazy lists too. Typically coupled with these questions are examinations of faith and spirituality. Where is God in all this? What really happens to us after we die? Where did your soulmate go? Some grieving soulmates find comfort in their faith, while others—even some who before the death felt strong in their faith—begin to flounder.

After the death of her middle-aged sister-in-law, Mary, followed closely by the unexpected death of Mary's husband, Mike, who was

Patti's brother and soulmate, Patti Stahl found herself floundering. "I really questioned my faith," she wrote. "I had a hard time believing God would allow this to happen. How could he allow four kids to be parentless in such a short time? How could he break so many people's hearts...and then again! The God I grew up loving and believing in was a kind and gentle God. How could he turn on me? Why couldn't he prevent this double whammy? Why did I feel so alone and empty? The God I loved was not there for me during my greatest pain. And I certainly didn't feel like he was 'carrying me.' Of the many trials and tribulations I have been through in my 52 years on earth, this was a huge hurdle for me—and I am a really bad jumper!"

> "The visual I have of the loss of my husband is like a bobbing sailboat in the ocean. Losing Wendell stopped the wind in our sails. Feelings of never finding my way back to reality set in. I now find the visual of a bobbing sailboat in the ocean as a calming reminder that rechanneling my life requires me to be patient. I need to stay on board and not make any rash decisions."
>
> — Katie LaPrairie

Most of us are really bad jumpers. Feelings of anger, betrayal, and doubt—sometimes targeted at God or specific religious beliefs, sometimes more generally philosophical and existential—often well up for grieving soulmates. This is normal and natural. "It's OK to be really angry at God," wrote Karen Goebel. "He can take it, and He gets it."

In their letters to me, several soulmates described moments in which they have received spiritual reassurance from their partners who died. Teri Gaglione was only a college student when her true love, George, suddenly and unexpectedly fell into a coma after a cerebral hemorrhage. He lingered in the hospital for ten days before he died. During George's viewing, Teri described that she "felt he was communicating to me that he was in a joyful, peaceful place. I still believe with all my heart that in our closeness, George was able to share his afterlife experience with me." Teri went on to become a licensed social worker and has worked in hospice care since 1979.

Marcia Teachout had a similar experience. "A few days after Steve passed away, I looked up toward the sky and asked Steve if he could somehow let me know that he was OK," she wrote. "The next morning when I was leaving the house to walk my dog, it was just starting to rain. It was strange because as I looked out across the park, the sun was shining brightly on the trees. I looked above me to find the rain clouds and there was a rainbow, which had long been a significant symbol in our relationship. Just as suddenly as the rain started, it stopped, and the rainbow disappeared."

> *"I struggle daily to find a new purpose, to follow the advice of caring friends, to live without Allen. I have found that it takes a tremendous effort to work at being OK, but my Allen's final words to me were, 'You're gonna be OK,' so that is my goal. We were so very fortunate to have been soulmates, and that love is not always the love felt between two people. I believe that those of us who loved and love in this fashion are fulfilled in a way that is beyond words."*
>
> — Judith Holtz

Karl Weaver felt a sense of release during his wife's memorial service. He was feeling angry about some relationship troubles when, "Suddenly she spoke to me. I don't mean that I heard anything audibly. It was a mental phenomenon, but there it was: she was telling me that she was sorry."

Outside of specific spiritual encounters, it is extremely common for grieving soulmates to believe that their partners are waiting for them in heaven. This viewpoint does not diminish the necessity or power of their grief, but it does typically give them a profound sense of hope. "I believe that John is my special angel who is watching over me," wrote Joanne Churilla. "He has visited me in dreams several times, and these are precious visits that I hang onto."

Finding meaning again, though, is largely about living out one's remaining days on earth with a sense of meaning and purpose. Faith and spirituality may provide a longer-term sense of assuredness and peace, but there still remains the critical question of why *today* matters. In other words, what will get you out of bed every morning? Penny Blazej found an answer in a new career. "I went from being a manager with IBM to working as a hospice volunteer and then re-educated myself to become a grief counselor," she wrote. "My soulmate put me on the right path, and I am forever grateful to her."

IDEAS FOR GRIEVING SOULMATES

Finding meaning in life again after the death of the one person who each day gave your life profound meaning is an extraordinarily daunting part of your quest for healing. You had a life you loved very much. Now that life has been destroyed. How do you go about building a new and different life, one in which you feel satisfied, even happy?

> *"For me, helping others made me feel better, and the connection you feel with others who are grieving is healing to your soul. The lingering 'why?' question will not be answered, but I feel like I found peace in helping others."*
>
> — Victoria Muñoz-Schmitt

First, you must remember to be heroically patient with yourself. For grieving soulmates, this tends to be a mourning need that you can only begin to take on substantively after months (and possibly years) of acknowledging the reality of the death and embracing the pain of the loss. In the early weeks and months after the death, it is wise to seek get-through-the-day meaning and comfort in small things. A cup of tea. A chat with someone who cares about you. A walk in the park. While such activities may not constitute Meaning with a capital M, that does not mean they are not essential to the reconstruction of your life. They are indeed.

Laura Renker found this to be true after the death of her soulmate, Les. She took solace in little things she could do to mourn and comfort herself each day—small steps that are not in and of themselves heroic but eventually add up to unstoppable momentum toward healing. "What has helped to keep his memory alive over the last four years has been the gentle powers of my strong Catholic faith, talking to him often about things that are happening, keeping bouquets of fresh flowers and photographs around the house, playing classical music, walking, and reading," she wrote. "I visit Les quite often at the cemetery close by, spend time with friends and family, wear his favorite ring, look at beautiful paintings, and travel to places we used to go and many new destinations as well. I try to practice daily prayer and meditation and most importantly, help other people whenever possible. Truly, these simple and uncomplicated gestures are leading me to a gradual sense of healing, peace, and reconciliation and giving me the necessary hope for living well into the future." Notice Laura's conscious and daily commitment to actively mourn.

Second, if and when you are ready, you may find you need to gently but consciously work on breaking free of some of the routines and habits that shaped your life with your soulmate. The fact that you were likely best friends imbued your time together with great meaning. But now that you are on your own, or "flying solo" as one church group I know for widows and widowers calls it, you may no longer find meaning in all of the rituals and activities you once shared. Learning to ask yourself, "What do *I* want to do today?" is part of this mourning need. Ditto, "Do I even enjoy _____ anymore?" Also, "Which people and places and objects and activities do I now feel drawn to?" Of course, grieving the routines and habits you may be leaving behind along the way is also part of this.

And third, you will find that there can be great reward in learning to trust in and love yourself as an individual child of God. One of my foundational beliefs is that each human life has purpose. Circumstances change, other precious people come and go, but still you are you and you are here. Your unique divine spark remains. Your divine spark is the ember of meaning and purpose that lives inside you. To be sure it has been dimmed by the death of your soulmate, but it still glimmers deep down. Your heroic mourning need here is to find and feed the flame. It may well take a great deal of time as well as heroic effort to learn to trust in your own intuition and capacity to find your way to a new sense of purpose.

Here are a two other soulmate skills you might consider turning to as you work on this challenging need:

SHARED VALUES

Meaning comes from living life according to values you cherish. It comes from what is called "congruency," which is a psychological term for behaving on the outside in alignment with how you think and feel on the inside.

If you are living congruently, you

- try to be honest at all times.
- are aware of who you really are and do not wear masks.
- honestly claim your thoughts and speak them.
- honestly claim your feelings and show them.
- honestly claim your mistakes and try to correct them.
- honestly claim your doubts and questions and raise them.
- honestly claim your beliefs and live them.

The shared values on which your soulmate relationship was built can help guide you in your heroic search for meaning. If they were the bedrock of your relationship, they can again serve as the bedrock of your mourning process.

What do you value in life? What are your bottom-line priorities? Heroically reaching out to connect with organizations, activities, and relationships that support these values and align with these priorities will help you re-establish meaning in your continued living.

Now, I understand that your answers to these questions may be shifting as a result of the death of your soulmate. If that is the case

"I began to ask myself some pretty hard questions. Was I really ready to give up? Was it true that I could not live without my husband, my other half, my soulmate? The day we met, something so recognizable settled in me, and I felt I had known him forever. But as his hand slipped from mine, and my body over his could not hold him to me, I wondered what on this lonely earth could motivate me ever again..?

I remembered wanting to go with him or even instead of him. Impossible. What would make me want to get up in the morning now? As I lay there, answers began to come. The word 'purpose' kept popping up. I needed a purpose, a reason to live, a reason that meant something special, a reason to get up in the morning.

Finding my purpose took some time, but it was time well spent. I knew it had to be outside 'me'. I knew it should benefit others. When I found my purpose, it started an entirely new life for me. I began teaching classes to seniors on Living with Joy. It gave me new joy as I tried to give it to others. It truly led me through my grief."

— Jean Brody

for you, rest assured that this process is normal and natural. Death forces us to reconsider all of our assumptions. That's why this heroic mourning need has the verb "search" in it. Most grievers spend a great deal of time and energy trying to figure out anew what will joyfully get them out of bed in the morning again.

Jo Anne Gregory chose to make the searching process as proactive as possible. "For many months after Gary's death," she wrote, "I attended grief support classes, read numerous books on grief and mourning, told my story over and over, attended seminars, and had monthly visits with some fantastic women who either have walked or are walking in my shoes. I encourage everyone experiencing a loss to read, talk, and pray."

Where did Jo Anne's search take her? "I long for the day that Gary and I will be together again," she said. "But in the meantime, I will honor Gary's memory by returning to volunteer work that we loved, assisting and visiting the aged and elderly in convalescent and hospice settings." Jo Anne's search for meaning took her back to the values she shared with her soulmate, Gary.

So did Rita Roush's. Since the death of her soulmate, she has clung to what she and Steve valued most—their family. "Thinking about our children and grandchildren has helped to drag me along," she wrote. "I had many thoughts of leaving this world myself because the pain was too much. But I knew I had to be both Nana and Papaw to our grandkids. Our own children had suffered a large enough loss already; I knew I had to be there for them also."

"I now understand that it is true, 'out of bad can come good.' The good is that I have faith in God, I recognize beauty more than ever, and I live fully, not taking anything for granted. As the result of my mother's death, I have been newly inspired in my nursing profession. I work with greater passion and purpose than ever before. I realize my career is indeed a calling; this is my purpose as I can recognize firsthand the joys of life and the darkness of death but also the beauty of God's mercy and goodness in all that He creates. I have hope, peace, and love in my heart that I have vowed to pass along to others who may have broken hearts."

— Michele Hackett

PRIVILEGE AND HONOR

The sense of privilege and honor you may have felt to be a soulmate can serve you well in heroically searching for new meaning in life. You were grateful. You can choose to continue to cultivate gratitude.

Keeping a gratitude journal is one tried and true method of appreciating the wonder and meaning of life. Taking a few minutes at the end of each day to jot down several things you experienced that day that you feel grateful for—small things and big things alike—helps put the spotlight on all the good that remains a part of your existence. Regularly writing thank-you notes or emails or letters of appreciation is another way to help yourself. Meditating with a focus on the things for which you are grateful is a third.

SOUL EYES

by Anne van Tonningen

Walking through green velvet hills,
I tell you aloud
Of the beauty I see
with my human eyes.
Resting in heaven's holy light,
You share the peacefulness
of the soul's life with me:
Love pure and eternal.

Studies show that cultivating gratitude improves physical and psychological health, fosters good sleep, improves self-esteem, increases mental strength, and enhances empathy. Don't all those transformative benefits seem like they're well worth a few minutes of your time every day?

Of course, cultivating gratitude never means repressing or denying your natural and necessary pain. As we have emphasized throughout this book, the hurt is justified and also demands your attention. Try to remember the power of "and." You can mourn the pain *and* cultivate gratitude for all the good things that were and are. You can feel torn apart *and* privileged to continue to be alive. These are not either/or propositions. Instead, they are the bittersweet reality of human life.

Please write about your search for meaning since your soulmate's death. Have your former beliefs changed at all? Where have you found new meaning, big or small?

CHAPTER NINE

HEROIC MOURNING NEED 6.

RECEIVE ONGOING
SUPPORT FROM
OTHERS

"*The great love is gone. There are still little loves—friend to friend, brother to sister, student to teacher. Will you deny yourself comfort at the hearthfire of a cottage because you may no longer sit by the fireplace of a palace? Will you deny yourself to those who reach out to you in hopes of warming themselves at your hearthfire?*"

— Mercedes Lackey

The quality and quantity of understanding support you receive from others during your grief journey will have a major influence on your capacity to heal. You cannot—nor should you try to—do this alone. The quest for healing is never a solo endeavor. It takes a company of travelers willing to join up and set off together. It takes the commitment of mutual support and friendship.

Drawing on the experiences and encouragement of friends, fellow mourners, and compassionate counselors is not a weakness but a healthy human need. And because heroic mourning is a process that takes place over a long period of time, this support must be available months and even years after the death of your soulmate.

"The first year as a widow was the hardest work ever. My family and friends were paramount in my survival. Now I am into the second year as a widow. I'm pleased that the hard work in year one has culminated in a priceless connection with my family and a recognition of the value of friends."

— Donna Thompson

Unfortunately, because our society places so much value on the ability to "carry on," "keep your chin up," and "keep busy," many mourners are abandoned by friends and family shortly after the event of the death. "It's over and done with" and "It's time to get on with your life" are the types of messages directed at mourners that still dominate. Obviously, these messages encourage you to deny or repress your grief rather than express it.

To be truly helpful, the people in your support system must appreciate the impact this death has had on you. They must understand that in order to heal, you must be allowed—even encouraged—to mourn long after the death. And they must encourage you to see mourning not as an enemy to be vanquished but as a necessity to be experienced as a result of having loved.

"The nicest, most supportive thing I've heard of to help a grieving person came to me through a California cousin after he lost his wife of many years. He told me that his sister asked him if she could just give him a quick phone call daily for a while. It could be at a time that my cousin chose, and when he got to feeling that he didn't need the daily contact any longer, then at his signal she would stop."

— Beverley Turnley

For grieving soulmates, however, this mourning need is often complicated by the nature of the soulmate relationship. It is not unusual for soulmates to isolate themselves. As a couple, they sometimes revel in and depend on each other so much that pre-existing or longtime outside relationships wither and potential new ones don't get made. So, surviving soulmates who relied heavily or nearly exclusively on their partners may find themselves lacking a good support system after the death. Has this happened to you?

Conversely, other grieving soulmates consciously or unconsciously spurn the help of friends and family. Unused to turning to anyone but their soulmate for emotional intimacy and support, they shut themselves down to outside help. "Loneliness set in, mostly by my own doing," wrote Jean Brody. "I got to the point where I did not want to continually tell friends how I was coping (or not), so it was easier to stay by myself in my house. I made up all sorts of reasons why I could not go out to lunch or stay overnight with family." Have you had this experience?

A caveat: Sometimes, especially in the early weeks and months of your grief, you may appropriately find it necessary to isolate yourself from others. Young grief invites you to turn inward, and during this time, you may feel the need to be alone. You may also find yourself annoyed at or irritated by random social overtures. Karen Goebel explains this phenomenon well:

People will approach you in odd places (grocery store, school) and expect you to share your feelings with them. They'll ask you how you are, and they'll tell you they are praying. They'll tell you they will do anything if you just ask. And all you want to do is get your groceries and get out of the store before you need to cry again. Sometimes it feels like they want you to cry. Like they want to be that shoulder for you. It's OK to tell them you are doing terrible. That your life is torn apart and you don't really want to talk about it right now. You don't need to feel like everyone deserves to be an intimate participant of your grief.

IDEAS FOR GRIEVING SOULMATES

After the early shock of grief begins to wear off and the normal and necessary inward-focused time of self-isolation has run its course, support groups and grief counseling are quite often extremely helpful lifelines for grieving soulmates. Remember, soulmate grief is naturally complicated and oversized. That means coping with it and encountering the six needs of mourning require extra helpings of everything.

Participating in a support group and seeing a grief counselor not only will provide you with extra empathy and support from your fellow human beings, it will help you embrace the other five needs of mourning as well. As you talk, listen, and feel in the safe presence of a compassionate counselor and/or support group, you will also be

"I have survived with the help of a wonderful counselor. With the help she gave me I have been able to start living again."

— Wilda Stauffer

acknowledging the reality of the death, embracing the pain of the loss, remembering the person who died, working on your new self-identity, and searching for meaning.

Kathe Klein is just one of many grieving soulmates who wrote to me about the importance of their grief support groups. "It is in the shelter of each other that we once again live, heal, and find our joy after a tremendous loss," she said. "It is in the security of this circle that the grip of loneliness and fear is loosened. There is a great promise of connection, a loving alliance of grief and hope. The cycle of giving (sharing) and receiving (listening) is very humbling. This is one of the group's quietest gifts. Those of us further along the path are reaching back for the hands of those just starting this journey. We become real friends because we understand, accept, and are able to share some painful experiences in our private lives…to open to each other in order to let in the light, love, and laughter."

"I am gaining comfort from attending a monthly grief support group. Talking to others who are going through the same situation has been very beneficial. Family, friends, church family, and even caring strangers are great assets in getting on with my life."

— Angela Parkins

You may even, at some point, take on the role of starting or facilitating a grief support group. After a long, slow period of normal and necessary just getting by, Denise Meehan did just that. "With the help of a grief support group, which I, along with another member, began facilitating eight years ago, my healing and a new chapter in my life began," she wrote. "Within my own loss, the sharing helped put things in perspective in the totally unfamiliar world of grief. We support each other sometimes with tears and other times with laughter. In this transformation of life I see things so differently. What matters is the kindness of others and embracing what is important each day."

That doesn't mean it's always easy to get started with a support group or counselor, however. Many people, raised in our culture of rugged individualism and stuffing emotions, are reluctant to share their very private, innermost thoughts and feelings out loud. If you are among them and have been reluctant to join a support group or see a counselor, rest assured that they are less scary than you imagine them to be. Muster the courage to try them for three to five sessions then decide if you want to continue. "I found it hard to go to support meetings in the beginning as it was so painful to talk about Ron's death," Lynda Moses wrote to me. "But the more I talked, the better I felt."

BEST FRIENDS

Your best-friend skills as a soulmate can help you foster old friendships and develop new ones, both of which will greatly help you heroically meet this mourning need.

Remember back in Chapter One when we went over the qualities of the best-friends relationship? Regular communication, mutual confiding, loyalty, shared decision-making, honesty, and forgiveness were among the attributes we covered. The gift of presence is also central.

I want you to consider these qualities as you figure out ways to actively move toward healing that work for you. As all mourners do, you need friendship. But as a grieving soulmate who is accustomed to best friendship, you may find that cultivating not only casual friendships but deep relationships with one or more people will provide you with the kind of soul-connection balm you need.

If you do not have good friends, believe that you can make them. After all, you're a soulmate! You know how to be the best friend that someone ever had! Draw upon your skills in communicating, confiding, loyalty, honesty, and presence. Yes, it takes time and effort to nurture new or flagging friendships, but that's why I've used the term "heroic" in this book. Your outsized grief demands the support of strong relationships, and as you know, strong relationships take commitment. And no, your new or revived close friends won't ever replace your best friend who died, but they can and will support you as you do the necessary work of mourning.

In Chapter Five I shared my thinking about the "rule of thirds"—one-third of the people in your life have the capacity to be supportive, one-third are neutral, and the remaining third are toxic to healing. In your proactive efforts to nurture strong friendships, be sure to concentrate on the first third.

Geralyn Nathe-Evans describes the first third in this way: "Those who are the greatest support honor my space, my journey, and my pain. They say his name, speak of the memories, and honor me to move at this pace of healing and reconciling all that was with what is and will be for the future."

Fellow grieving soulmates who also fall into the first third, especially, have the potential to become one of your new best friends. After all, who understands the soulmate relationship better than another soulmate? "My biggest piece of advice I would share with others is that it is important to talk with someone who has suffered a similar loss," wrote Rita Roush. "They can validate your feelings, and they understand what you are going through. People were trying to encourage me by saying time will help, but I didn't really believe them until I heard it from another young widow."

Finally, it doesn't take a posse of new best friends to meet your needs for strong human connection. As you know, just one really good friend can mean the difference between hope and despair. Keep this in mind as you work to open yourself to and build relationships.

COMPANIONSHIP

The support of at least one close, strong relationship is central to healing your soulmate grief, but outside of that relationship, regular contact and companionship with a cast of casual friends is also important. We as human beings are built to interact with one another. Studies of prisoners in solitary confinement show profound and long-term psychological damage. The movie *Castaway* dramatizes what happens when a person is isolated for too long—he invents a companion, in this case the volleyball named Wilson.

It is likely that you enjoyed and depended on the daily companionship you shared with your soulmate. Recognizing this, you must now find and connect to other people with whom to share your days.

When you are ready, proactively and heroically seeking companionship in various ways will help you heal and find your new sweet spot of meaning in life. Getting involved in volunteer organizations, neighborhood goings-on, clubs, groups at your place of worship, sports, and other leisure activities will help you in many ways, but establishing regular human contact is the most important one.

How much regular human contact do you need? The extroverts among you will likely benefit from a wide social circle, while the

> *"After moving, through church and new neighbors, I found that just talking about my loss was such a relief. I didn't know that I needed to talk. The new friends just walked beside me, let me cry, let me say the same things over and over. I was slowly beginning to heal. The griefbursts kept happening; they still do five years later. But that sharing really started my journey of healing."*
>
> — Dorlene Szetela

> *"I kept telling myself things would get better, but they never seemed to improve until one day recently, I decided that if he were here, he wouldn't want me so sad all the time. I embraced a special occasion and spent it with a family I barely knew. I had fun! I laughed. I cried! As I went home from this occasion, I said out loud, 'I did it!' I went out, and although he was always on my mind, I laughed and enjoyed the new company."*
>
> — Karen Steen

introverts among you may only need one or two close friends and a few occasional companions to feel sufficiently connected and supported. And the time you spend with others doesn't have to be vast for it to help. One grieving soulmate offered a simple but powerful tip: "When days seem impossible, I sometimes call a friend just to chat for a few minutes about most anything. They don't realize the reason."

Of course, social support is not a panacea. It does not replace the more inward-focused mourning needs and by itself is not enough. "Surrounded by loving friends and family, I continue to have the feeling of being so alone, so less-than while literally surrounded by people," wrote Geralyn Nathe-Evans. If you, too, experience Geralyn's feeling of aloneness in the midst of others, I encourage you to understand the loneliness as a symptom of your ongoing grief that needs more exploration and expression. Acknowledge it, feel it, embrace it, write about it, yell about it if you want to, and yes, talk to others about it. A good support group or grief counselor will not be offended by your feeling of aloneness and will support you in working through it.

Vera Hummel said that when it came to companionship and other needs of mourning, she learned what worked for her through a period of trial and error. "I rejected all suggestions of 'how I should grieve,' most offers to attend grief therapy, and others' suggestions about what I was likely to be feeling or experiencing," she wrote. "I accepted invitations that were meaningful with people that I respected, and I did only what I felt I was able to do with dignity. I spoke openly and honestly with those in my circle of love and compassionate support, and I did eventually come to understand that there were some things about his death and my grief that did not need to be shared. As he lived, my husband taught me how to live, how to love, and how to serve. He would have said to speak the truth, kindly, and to the right people."

Please write about your support system and your willingness to ask for and accept the empathy of others.

CHAPTER TEN

REACHING THE GOAL OF YOUR QUEST—
RECONCILIATION

"I didn't know it at the time, but by allowing myself to authentically grieve, I was walking the road to reconciliation. I will never 'recover' from the loss of this man I loved so much and who left this world entirely too soon. But I can honor him by living on and making sure that his legacy lives on. My heart will always bear the scars of the love I lost. They are ugly and large. But grieving authentically has allowed for the pieces that once littered the floor to be put back together like some kind of heart puzzle. I miss him every day. My love for him is still immense. He helps me to carry on, to live and love as fully as my patchwork heart can."

— Megan Quinn

The grieving soulmate's quest to mourn heroically in order to rebuild a life of love and meaning is an ambitious one—but for those of you who learned and mastered the soulmate skills before embarking, it is also one within reach.

When you committed to this quest in Chapter Two, I asked you to choose between two paths. I asked you to choose either doing the admittedly arduous and painful work of fully encountering and expressing your soulmate grief so that you could learn to find meaning in life again OR living a shadow-life for the remainder of your days, grieving deeply inside but not heroically mourning and never really, truly, and fully engaging with life again.

If you are still here with me in Chapter Ten, I presume that you chose the first path. If so, I extend you my heartfelt congratulations and admiration. Even if you are still in the midst of your quest, you are to be recognized. Because, despite its epic and life-affirming rewards, heroic mourning is harrowing.

Some of you may be far enough along in your quest to catch glimpses of your ultimate destination, however. I call it "reconciliation." Other psychological grief models call it "resolution," "recovery," "re-establishment," or "reorganization"—terms I don't like because they imply a state of finality.

You see, deep grief—like its conjoined twin, deep love—never truly ends. People do not "get over" grief. My personal and professional experience tells me that a total return to "normalcy" after the death of someone loved, let alone a soulmate, is not possible; we are all forever changed by the experience of loss.

No, we don't "get over" grief, but if we do the hard work of mourning, we can learn to reconcile it. Reconciling means integrating our new reality of moving forward in life without the physical presence of the person who died. Not just surviving, but really living, even thriving. With reconciliation comes a renewed sense of energy and confidence, an ability to fully acknowledge the reality of the death, and a capacity to become re-involved in the activities of living. There is also an acknowledgment that pain and grief are difficult, yet necessary, parts of life.

As the experience of reconciliation unfolds, you will recognize that life is and will continue to be dramatically different without the presence of your soulmate. We come to reconciliation in our grief journeys when the full reality of the death becomes a part of us. Beyond an intellectual working through of the death, there is also an emotional and spiritual working through. What had been understood at the "head" level is now understood at the "heart" level.

> *"It's been three years since his death. (It will be four years on March 19, 2016, at 8:52 p.m.) In the world of non-grievers, that sounds like a really, really long time. To them I most certainly must be 'over it' by now. Life goes on—blah, blah, blah."*
>
> — Beverley Turnley

To choose the path that leads to reconciliation requires that you first *descend*, not *transcend*. You don't get to go around or above or below your grief. You must go through it. And while you are going through it, you must also find ways to continually express it—heroically mourn it—if you are to integrate it into your being.

You will find that as you begin to reach your goal of reconciliation, the sharp, ever-present pain of grief will give rise to a renewed sense of meaning and purpose. Your feelings of loss will never completely disappear, of course, yet they will soften, and the intense pangs of grief will become less frequent. Hope for a continued life will emerge as you are able to make commitments to the future, realizing that your soulmate will never be forgotten but that your life can and must continue. The unfolding of this journey is not intended to create a return to an "old normal" but instead the discovery of a "new normal."

To help you explore where you might be on the path to reconciliation, the following criteria that suggest healing may be helpful. You don't have to check each item on the list for healing to be taking place. Reconciliation is an ongoing process. In fact, if you are early in your work of heroic mourning, you may not yet meet any of these criteria. Regardless, this list will give you a way to monitor your movement toward healing and trust that if you are working on your six needs of heroic mourning, you are on the right path.

SIGNS OF RECONCILIATION

As you embrace your grief and do the work of mourning, you can and will be able to demonstrate the majority of the following:

- [ ] A recognition of the reality and finality of the death.
- [ ] A return to stable eating and sleeping patterns.
- [ ] A renewed sense of release from the person who has died. You will have thoughts about your soulmate, but you will not be preoccupied by these thoughts.
- [ ] The capacity to enjoy experiences in life that are normally enjoyable.
- [ ] The establishment of new and healthy relationships.
- [ ] The capacity to live a full life without feelings of guilt or lack of self-respect.
- [ ] The drive to organize and plan your life toward the future.

☐ The serenity to become comfortable with the way things are rather than attempting to make things as they were.

☐ The versatility to welcome more change in your life.

☐ The awareness that you have challenged yourself to mourn heroically—and you have survived.

☐ The awareness that you do not "get over" your grief; instead, you have a new reality, meaning, and purpose in your life.

☐ The acquaintance with new parts of yourself that you have discovered in your grief journey.

☐ The adjustment to new role changes that have resulted from the loss of your soulmate relationship.

☐ The acknowledgment that the pain of loss in an inherent part of life resulting from the ability to give and receive love.

Reconciliation does not happen all at once. Instead, it emerges much in the way grass grows. Usually we don't check our lawns daily to see if the grass is growing, but it does grow and soon we come to realize it's time to mow the grass again. Likewise, we don't look at ourselves each day as mourners to see how we are healing. Yet we do come to realize, over the course of months and years, that we have come a long way.

One of my greatest teachers, C. S. Lewis, wrote in *A Grief Observed* about his grief symptoms as they eased on his journey to reconciliation. "There was no sudden, striking, and emotional transition," he wrote. "Like the warming of a room or the coming of daylight, when you first notice them they have already been going on for some time."

On the path to healing, there usually is not one great moment of "arrival" but rather a myriad of subtle changes and small advancements. It's helpful to have gratitude for every baby step along the way. If you are beginning to taste your food again, be thankful. If you mustered the energy to meet your friend for lunch, be grateful.

If you finally got a good night's sleep, rejoice.

Of course, you will also take steps backward from time to time on the path to healing, but that is to be expected. Keep believing in yourself. Recommit each day to your quest to reconcile your grief and have hope that you can and will come to live and love fully again.

Where do you see yourself right now on the path to reconciliation? What progress have you made so far, and what hopes and goals do you have for ongoing reconciliation?

WORKING TOWARD WHOLEHEARTEDNESS

Flip back to the torn paper heart on this book's front cover. Your heart has been torn in two by the death of your soulmate, but through heroic mourning, you are working on stitching it back together.

"I think our capacity for wholeheartedness can never be greater than our willingness to be brokenhearted. It means engaging with the world from a place of vulnerability and worthiness."

— Brené Brown

Your goal is wholeheartedness. According to author Brené Brown, wholehearted people believe in living with courage, compassion, and connection. They make themselves vulnerable and open because they value authenticity. Instead of resisting change and the sometimes chaotic nature of life, they learn to surrender to whatever is happening that may be outside their control. They develop the skills of living in the moment and positivity. They find beauty and meaning in the imperfection of humanity doing and being and loving the best it can.

You began this quest from a place of brokenheartedness. Of course your heart was broken. Your soulmate was torn away from you. But then the question became, "What do I do with this broken heart?" And you found the courage to answer the question nobly and heroically. "If I fully experience and express my grief, finding ways to do so that are as big and as wide as the love we shared," you said, "I believe I can put my heart back together. To do so is to honor my soulmate. It is also to affirm that I, as an individual child of God, am worthy. It is to attest that my life is precious and that I believe in living and loving as fully as I can until I, too, take my last breath."

The more open, honest, expressive, congruent, and present you are each day, the more wholehearted you will become. Reconciliation in grief is a place of wholeheartedness. Your heart is a patchwork, to be sure, but when you dedicate yourself to heroic mourning, you can trust it will once again be whole. And in the imperfection you can find beauty and meaning.

Some of you may be doubting your ability to become wholehearted again. If you are, I understand. At various points on the path to reconciliation you will likely find yourself exhausted and in despair. Your quest for healing is so hard—maybe the hardest thing you've ever done. It's normal to want to give up now and then.

Others of you may be having a hard time mustering the desire to work toward wholeheartedness. You may be so deep in the wound of your grief that you don't have the energy to climb out. Besides, you may ask, isn't the idea of wholeheartedness simply a folly that implies that you don't really need your soulmate who died?

But you are a soulmate! Soulmates live by values! They revel in the joys of friendship and companionship, including physical contact. They understand the rewards of vulnerability, kindness, perseverance, and selflessness. They have a sense of adventure as well as a sense of humor. They embrace ritual. And they are grateful. When you are at your best, you do and are all of these things.

I have absolutely no doubt that you have the capacity to become wholehearted again. If you are struggling with mustering the desire to become wholehearted again, you may simply need some extra help with your normal and necessary depression of grief.

The spiritual activist Marianne Williamson famously said, "Our deepest fear is not that we are inadequate. Our deepest fear is that we are powerful beyond measure." I believe that grieving soulmates harbor untold power but are often afraid to tap into it. If you are resisting embracing your profound grief and heroically mourning, you are doing so from a place of fear. Making yourself vulnerable is scary. Befriending your deepest pain and darkest thoughts and feelings is frightening. The only way to overcome your fear and tap your soulmate powers for healing is to make yourself vulnerable, open, and expressive. Try to embody these three adjectives in at least one small way, every day, one day at a time.

Please write about your quest for a new wholeheartedness.

RELIGHTING YOUR DIVINE SPARK

Earlier in the book we talked about your divine spark, which is the ember of meaning and purpose that lives inside you. Your soulmate helped your divine spark shine bright, and now his or her death has naturally dimmed it. You may even feel that when your soulmate died, your divine spark was extinguished.

The process of heroic mourning relights your divine spark. It's kind of counterintuitive, really. Immersing yourself in and surrendering to death, grief, and mourning is what gives you new life. You might think you can go straight to the relighting—checking out new activities, dating again, making an effort to have fun. But it doesn't work that way. Trying to skip your normal and necessary period of darkness will only make you unhappier for longer and set you up for a zombified kind of existence.

The best legacy you can create for your soulmate is one in which you work on the six needs of mourning in heroic ways and eventually find your way to reconciliation and relight your unique divine spark. Your soulmate deserves it, and you deserve it. To do anything less is to sell yourself and your soulmate short.

Which activities or practices give you a sense of purpose, peace, or joy? What nurtures your soul? How to relight your divine spark can be found in your answers to these questions.

LOVING AGAIN

Throughout this book I have encouraged you to heroically mourn so that one day you might live and love fully again. Earlier in this chapter I listed reconciliation criteria that included the capacity to enjoy experiences in life, the drive to organize and plan your life toward the future, and the establishment of new and healthy relationships. These are perhaps your most important goals in your quest.

Does this mean you need to eventually seek out another soulmate, spouse, or intimate relationship?

No, I don't believe it does. What it does mean is that love and human connection are the greatest gifts of life and that to choose to live without love is to choose to die while you are still alive. The death of your soulmate has created a huge void in your life. To the extent that it can be filled again, love is the only thing that can fill it. Your work of heroic mourning will open you to foster old relationships and develop new ones. These relationships will never replace your soulmate, but they can give your life meaning again.

If you use your soulmate skills to reach out and connect, you may strengthen existing relationships with children, grandchildren, siblings, extended family members, old friends, neighbors, coworkers, fellow volunteers, and others. Through the process of developing your new self-identity and searching for meaning, you might also make new friends. Don't worry about the quantity of relationships you work on; concern yourself with the quality. As you learned from being a soulmate, close relationships are everything.

Some of you will find another soulmate, though. I myself have always believed that each of us has three soulmates somewhere out there in the world, but on a planet of seven-and-a-half billion people, it's hard to find them. Potential soulmates are rare. If you do find yourself developing a soulmate relationship with someone new (as a number of the grieving soulmates who wrote to me said they were fortunate to do), I support you and am happy for you. I also hope you will continue to heroically mourn the death of your first soulmate whenever grief thoughts and feelings arise, which they will naturally continue to do.

Whether learning to live and love fully again for you means fostering close relationships with friends and family or finding a new partner, I am hoping you will agree that love is well worth the risk. Yes, loving again means agreeing to grieve again one day, but such is the paradox of human life.

Love is worth it. It is always worth it. In fact, it's the only thing that's worth anything.

Who do you love or care about? In what ways are you nurturing relationships with these people? If you need more love in your life, how are you reaching out to make new connections?

A FINAL WORD

The grieving soulmates who wrote to me entrusted me with their precious stories. I cannot thank them enough for sharing what they have learned about grief, mourning, and healing. Their struggles and triumphs alike stand as beacons of hope for those of you embarking on your quest for healing.

If you would like to share your soulmate story or tips for healing after the death of a soulmate for a future edition of this book, I hope you will write to me at drwolfelt@centerforloss.com.

Right now, I invite you to close your eyes and picture the smiling face of your beloved soulmate. Take a few minutes to make yourself vulnerable to whatever thoughts and feelings arise for you. Then reach out to someone who cares about you and tell them what's going on inside you. Use words and gestures that are as quiet or as powerful as your feelings.

This small act of great mourning is a step. Countless more steps lie before you on your heroic quest. But you set off with a soulmate's heart and training, so I know you are equal to the task. I wish you Godspeed.

USING THIS BOOK IN A SOULMATE GRIEF SUPPORT GROUP
This book can be used as a foundational text for a support group for grieving soulmates.

I recommend that a counselor or trained layperson whose own loss is not recent facilitate the group. For additional guidance, those who have never led a grief support group might also want to review my book entitled *The Understanding Your Grief Support Group Guide: Starting and Leading a Bereavement Support Group*. Or, better yet, come join us in Colorado for my seminar entitled Support Group Facilitator Training. For details, visit centerforloss.com and click on Trainings.

Meeting once a week for a period of several months allows for good continuity and momentum. Here is a possible 12-meeting structure:

MEETING 1
Introductions and brief story sharing. Pass out copies of the book to all participants for use beginning at the next meeting.
HOMEWORK FOR MEETING 2: *Read the Preface and Introduction and fill out the journal sections in the Introduction.*

MEETING 2
Discuss the Introduction and the journal responses.
HOMEWORK FOR MEETING 3: *Read Chapter One and fill out the journal sections in that chapter.*

MEETING 3
Discuss Chapter One and the journal responses.
HOMEWORK FOR MEETING 4: *Read Chapter Two and fill out the journal sections in that chapter.*

MEETING 4
Discuss Chapter Two and the journal responses.
HOMEWORK FOR MEETING 5: *Read Chapter Three and fill out the journal sections in that chapter.*

MEETING 5
Discuss Chapter Three and the journal responses.
HOMEWORK FOR MEETING 6: *Read Chapter Four and fill out the journal sections in that chapter.*

MEETING 6
Discuss Chapter Four and the journal responses.
HOMEWORK FOR MEETING 7: *Read Chapter Five and fill out the journal sections in that chapter.*

MEETING 7
Discuss Chapter Five and the journal responses.
HOMEWORK FOR MEETING 8: *Read Chapter Six and fill out the journal sections in that chapter.*

MEETING 8
Discuss Chapter Six and the journal responses.
HOMEWORK FOR MEETING 9: *Read Chapter Seven and fill out the journal sections in that chapter.*

MEETING 9
Discuss Chapter Seven and the journal responses.
HOMEWORK FOR MEETING 10: *Read Chapter Eight and fill out the journal sections in that chapter.*

MEETING 10
Discuss Chapter Eight and the journal responses.
HOMEWORK FOR MEETING 11: *Read Chapter Nine and fill out the journal sections in that chapter.*

MEETING 11
Discuss Chapter Nine and the journal responses.
HOMEWORK FOR MEETING 12: *Read Chapter Ten and fill out the journal sections in that chapter.*

MEETING 12
Discuss Chapter Ten and the journal responses. Discuss next steps. Hold a brief closing ceremony.

TRAINING AND SPEAKING ENGAGEMENTS

To contact Dr. Wolfelt about speaking engagements
or training opportunities at his Center for Loss and Life
Transition, email him at DrWolfelt@centerforloss.com.
Visit centerforloss.com for more information.

ALSO BY ALAN WOLFELT

Grief One Day at a Time: 365 Meditations to Help You Heal After Loss

After a loved one dies, each day can be a struggle. But each day, you can also find comfort and understanding in this daily companion. With one brief entry for every day of the calendar year, this little book by beloved grief counselor Dr. Alan Wolfelt offers small, one-day-at-a-time doses of guidance and healing.

ISBN 978-1-61722-238- 2 • 384 pages • softcover • $14.95

Healing a Spouse's Grieving Heart: 100 Practical Ideas After Your Husband or Wife Dies

This guide offers 100 practical, here-and-now suggestions for helping widowers and widows mourn well so they can go on to live well again. Whether your spouse died recently or long ago, you will find comfort and healing in this compassionate book.

ISBN 978-1-879651-37-1 • 128 pages • softcover • $11.95

ALL DR. WOLFELT'S PUBLICATIONS CAN BE ORDERED BY MAIL FROM:
Companion Press | 3735 Broken Bow Road | Fort Collins, CO 80526
(970) 226-6050 | www.centerforloss.com

ALSO BY ALAN WOLFELT

Loving from the Outside In, Mourning from the Inside Out

Recognizing how the need to grieve is anchored in one's capacity to love, this calming guide contends that the act of mourning is healthy—and necessary—following a life-changing loss. Exploring the essential principles of love as well as the reasons behind it, this heartfelt handbook makes it possible to embrace grief and healing.

ISBN 978-1-61722-147- 7 • 128 pages • hardcover • $15.95

The Journey Through Grief: Reflections on Healing
SECOND EDITION

This revised, second edition takes Dr. Wolfelt's popular book of reflections and adds space for guided journaling, asking readers thoughtful questions about their unique mourning needs and providing room to record responses.

ISBN 978-1-879651-11-1

152 pages • hardcover • $21.95

ALL DR. WOLFELT'S PUBLICATIONS CAN BE ORDERED BY MAIL FROM:
Companion Press | 3735 Broken Bow Road | Fort Collins, CO 80526
(970) 226-6050 | www.centerforloss.com